BRITISH THEATRE DESIGN

DESIGN

THE MODERN AGE

BRITISH THEATRE DESIGN

THE MODERN AGE

Edited by JOHN GOODWIN
Foreword by PETER HALL

 PHOENIX ILLUSTRATED

THE WELTKUNST FOUNDATION ZÜRICH

HALF–TITLE PAGE: Poster design by John Byrne for Robert Holman's **Other Worlds**
(Royal Court, London, 1982).
DESIGNER JOHN BYRNE
(*Collection Max Stafford-Clark and Ann Pennington*)

FRONTISPIECE: Production photograph by Alex von Koettlitz of Berlioz's **The Trojans**
(Part 1) with Kristine Ciesinski as Cassandra (Opera North, 1987).
DESIGNERS TOM CAIRNS and ANTONY McDONALD

THIS PAGE AND FACING: Drawing by Pamela Howard for the first and last scenes of
Shakespeare's **The Taming of the Shrew**, staged in the traverse (Royal Shakespeare
Company tour, 1985).
DESIGNER PAMELA HOWARD

PREFACE (PAGE 11):   Costume design by William Dudley for a slave driver in Mozart's
Die Entführung (Glyndebourne, 1980).
DESIGNER WILLIAM DUDLEY
(*Collection Robert Pennant-Jones*)

first published by
WEIDENFELD & NICOLSON
with the support of
THE WELTKUNST FOUNDATION
and in association with
THE SOCIETY OF BRITISH THEATRE DESIGNERS

The Society of British Theatre Designers was founded in 1971 by John Bury, with Ralph Koltai,
Nicholas Georgiadis and Timothy O'Brien. It started life simply as a negotiating body, dealing with
managements and unions. Since then it has developed and diversified, and now has a membership
of more than two hundred. It aims to enhance the standing of British theatre design at home and
abroad in many different ways. One of these is to organize every four years a London exhibition of
theatre design which in part represents Britain in Prague at the International Quadriennale.
Designers are easily isolated by their work. Their society puts them in touch with one another,
with painters and sculptors, and with those working in theatre in other countries.

THE WEDDING FEAST

ACKNOWLEDGEMENTS

The publishers and editor thank, above all, the many photographers whose work appears in this book; but for them it would never have happened. Warm thanks are also of course due to the designers themselves. The great professionalism and care of Sarah Sears and Lindsey Rhodes were a constant strength during production of the book. The staff in theatres and libraries who provided pictures and information are too many to mention individually but their help is remembered, as is the kindness of those who allowed designs from their private collections to be published. Nicholas Payne of Opera North and Brian McMaster of the Welsh National Opera were good enough, at the request of John Higgins, to read through the typescript of his article. The captions to the pictures in the Dance section were ably compiled by Jane Pritchard. Lyn Haill's expert help with proof-reading was an act of true friendship.

The idea for this book
came from

ADRIAN WARD-JACKSON

to whom it is dedicated
with gratitude

Text © 1989, The Weltkunst Foundation
'The Years Before' © 1989, Roy Strong

First published in Great Britain in 1989
by George Weidenfeld & Nicolson Ltd
in association with the Society of British Theatre Designers

First published in paperback in 1991
by George Weidenfeld & Nicolson Ltd

Reprinted in 1992
Reprinted in 1995

This paperback edition first published in 1998 by
Phoenix Illustrated
Orion Publishing Group, Orion House
5, Upper St. Martin's Lane
London WC2H 9EA

British Library Cataloguing-in-Publication Data
A catalogue record for this book is available from
the British Library

ISBN 0753801299

Designed by Lindsey Rhodes
Typeset by Keyspools Ltd, Golborne, Lancashire
Printed and bound in Italy by L.E.G.O., Vicenza

CONTENTS

PREFACE

Before starting work on this book I had thought of it as no more than a most intriguing commission, and one that at the same time was worrying. But as it took shape it became a passion; so much so that at times a proper detachment was difficult. There has never before been a book on modern British theatre design, and breaking new ground was not just exhilarating, it was seductive.

The reason I was worried seemed at first, in my mind anyway, to threaten the entire project. Theatre designers are not careful collectors of their own original work. Nor do they go to great pains to have it recorded photographically. They are also as profligate as they are modest: costume designs are given away to friends, even lost; set models are not re-assembled after being broken down when the real thing is constructed. Still more alarming, camera shots of productions on stage seldom focus on the overall picture, concentrating rather on the actors' faces; and though these can express rage, love, grief, despair, joy – all humanity – with striking beauty, they were not what we wanted. How, therefore, were we to get sufficient, good, visual material?

It turned out that the problem was not so much whether it existed but how to track it down. The clever, indefatigable researcher for the book, Amelia Gatacre, had early on written to nearly 270 designers, but the response was disappointing. Our hunt pressed on with telephone calls beyond number, and almost daily visits to studios, theatres, homes, workrooms. Our appetite for material was as ferocious as hungry wolves for food. Finally – after many gruelling months – we had accumulated more than I ever imagined possible and far, far more than we could use. Amelia's small flat was no longer a place in which she could comfortably live her life, though she uncomplainingly did. It was a cluttered storeroom piled everywhere with masses of photographs and artwork – largely the designers' own choice of what best represented their work.

Selecting the pictures was often painfully difficult. Also, it quickly became apparent that designs which may have been brilliantly effective on stage were very occasionally not those which would look good on the page: the old dilemma of showing in one form work created for another. This dilemma is particularly acute when presenting on paper a single aspect of a three-dimensional art – theatre – which is also collaborative, with many different and mutually supporting elements. The only answer was to follow the demands of the form being used: that of a book.

When deciding the order of designers in each picture section it was found that an alphabetical arrangement did not work visually. So they are placed, where possible, in the same sequence as their names appear in the articles introducing each section. If their names are not mentioned in these articles, their work goes wherever it looks best.

The writers of the nine articles had a totally free hand on their given subjects, and if they wished to be critical they were certainly not discouraged. One view is sometimes contradicted by another. I welcome that.

The captions are full. I wanted every picture to be seen in a proper context and with the designers' own comments. In the interests of simplicity only composers – the main source – accompany opera titles, and only choreographers dance titles. Credits for the writers and composers of musicals are so abstruse it seemed safest to name everybody. In all captions the year mentioned is the one in which the production was first staged.

The book does not aim to promote any theory or to have any continuous theme. Its purpose – as the first of its kind – is to demonstrate the vitality of British theatre design here and abroad, chiefly during the uniquely productive decade preceding its publication. Through the work of more than 130 contemporary designers, it embraces a rich eclecticism imposed naturally, that is to say by the material we had gathered or were given. It is a kaleidoscopic vision – perhaps surprising and I hope revealing.

John Goodwin
London, 1989

JANNISARY SLAVE DRIVER
"ENTFÜHRUNG" GLYNDEBOURNE 1980
William Dudley.

11

FOREWORD

PETER HALL

The comic mask and the tragic mask are the traditional emblems of the theatre; and the actor knows how they affect him. Put on the comic mask, and no amount of weeping or hand-wringing will make it express grief; put on the tragic mask and laughter seems wrong and jokes unfunny.

The truly liberating mask of the theatre is, as the Greeks knew, neutral. The absence of an absolute statement frees it to express whatever mood the actor generates. The same, I believe, is true of good stage design. There has to be a neutrality about it which can allow the story its fullest realization.

It is a cliché that it is impossible to play comedy against a dark set. To laugh, the audience need lightness and brightness. To his contemporaries, there was nothing gloomy about the revolutionary naturalistic sets of Ibsen's dramas. But to us this historical Ibsen is oppressive; when designers pursue it they make a world where Ibsen's black comedy and penetrating irony can have little effect.

So stage design should support every mood, but not pre-empt it. It also mustn't do the work of the storyteller. If Macbeth's castle is designed exactly to match Shakespeare's words describing it, then the speech itself is superfluous.

Of all our senses sight is the sharpest – and the one that is particularly alert in today's world of television and exotic graphics. It therefore follows that no script, however good, and no band of performers, however talented, can surmount a design which contradicts the meaning of the play, opera or ballet.

For me, the ideal stage design for a play provides an environment which allows the meaning of the work to be expressed in all its contradictions, and which releases the actors' creativity. Even the proportions of a set, where the exits and entrances are located, whether the stage is raked, influence not only the visual impression of the play but the physical life of the actors. They need to believe in the world they inhabit, and to feel at ease within it.

The most organic way to discover this world is for the designer to work with the director and the actors in rehearsal for some weeks before anything at all is designed. The actors can then discover, with the director, the physical needs of the play; and the designer can, by watching the scenes develop, reach decisions about colour, atmosphere and texture. One of my happiest times in the theatre was directing the Judi Dench/Anthony Hopkins *Antony and Cleopatra*. We had rehearsed for a month, with the designer, Alison Chitty, sketching obsessively, before any models were made or any costume decisions taken. Such circumstances are rare, however. With this production, at the National Theatre in London, there was the luxury of twelve weeks' rehearsal. Normally, because of deadlines, budgeting, contractors' time, and other pressures, the design has to be ready even before rehearsals begin, with a danger that it is not organic but imposed.

Who starts the process of design, the director or the designer? My experience is that it can be either. For example, I have worked happily with the great John Bury for nearly thirty years on innumerable shows. I talk to him briefly about my subjective feelings on the play and the production, perhaps with some historical background if it is a period piece. From then on either of us may suggest the starting point. Sometimes it is an object; sometimes it is a texture or a colour. Often it is a material. The whole of our RSC *Wars of the Roses* cycle in the Sixties revolved around steel – its texture and brightness and its capacity to rust. This came from looking at the swords and weapons in Warwick Castle's armoury. Steel gave us a dangerous metal world – a place of power politics and sudden coups – and a metal floor on which the tramp of Fascist feet sounded as the cycle proceeded to the tyranny of *Richard III*.

The starting point can also be a period or a painter. For the opera *Salomé* it seemed to me as its director that the whole of Strauss's sensual shifting world – with its glittering chromaticisms – changes as mysteriously as the changing light of the moon, and it is the moon which dominates the piece. So I suggested the Secessionist painters, and particularly Klimt, to John. What he achieved was, to my eyes, a design that 'looked' like the music. I do not believe any opera design ever succeeds unless it expresses the music, or any play design that contradicts the style of the words. Modern abstract design does not seem to me to express Verdi, nor modern dress the Renaissance passions of Shakespeare. It is not necessary to be archaeologically 'correct', but there must be an acknowledgement – however selective and remote – of the period in which the piece was written.

Sketches of the design can be an interesting pointer for the next stage of the journey. An actor exists in three dimensions, however, and I prefer that to be evident from the start, the set evolving through a series of models, sometimes as many as four or five. But there always has to come a time, happily later rather than sooner, when design work is frozen to allow the set to be built and the costumes to be made. In the workshops, the designer can adjust colour and texture and the process of evolution in that way is still going on, but the basic decisions have by now usually been made.

When the set has arrived on stage, and the actors begin to rehearse in it, all sorts of design adjustments are again possible. The lighting, too, has to be plotted. Rightly, designers think of lighting as the final part of the overall design – a way not only of making the actor visible (for if you cannot see you cannot hear) but also of creating a mood, deepening the meaning of the play, and evoking a particular response from the audience. A design is not alive until it is lit.

In the last lunatic days of technical rehearsals when the lighting, the music, the costumes and the set are all put together in a seemingly impossible jumble of problems, the director and designer must keep their objectivity at all costs. During this time everything needs to be tested. The shape, the colour, the form of every minute of the play must be challenged. Nothing should be emphasized unless it has meaning; indeed nothing, in my view, should be there *unless* it has meaning.

Once I went to the dress rehearsal at the National of a most striking production by Michael Bogdanov of *The Mayor of Zalamea*. The set was a fascinating and quite remarkable structure of scaffolding. The actors moved in and out of it as if they were locked in a perilous cage. Brilliant though it was, it had little to do with the atmosphere of the play and actually limited the actors physically in a way which was distinctly unhelpful. As his producer, I suggested to Michael that he should do away with the set and give the piece on a bare stage, throwing into relief the speed and elegance of the text. He agreed, and his re-staging next morning went quickly and easily. It was the only time I have known such extreme cutting in thirty-five years in the theatre. And there were quite a few shocked mutterings at the expense. But we had done the right thing: the production worked.

Such inevitable and painful discoveries do fairly frequently come to light at dress rehearsals and previews. When I directed Tennessee Williams's *Orpheus Descending*, Alison Chitty created a wonderful, surrealistic set which, though still naturalistic enough for the action of the play, could lift off into something much more abstract to support the lyrical, non-naturalistic passages of the writing. But the costumes we had evolved were naturalistic, and at the first preview it became clear that the set and costumes simply did not work together. The costumes had to be lifted so that they too had a strong surrealistic quality. Last minute physical alterations of this kind may not come cheap, but they are often essential. Accountants and producers are inclined to think that changes of mind are the result of lack of preparation or of wilfulness. They are not. Change is part of the creative collaboration of the theatre.

A designer does more than design. He or she is the helpmate and critic of the director. When I think of the productions I have done, it is the designers of whom I think first because they guided me and the actors on our journey. I think of Leslie Hurry, Boris Aronson, Lila de Nobili, John Bury, Jocelyn Herbert, Bill Dudley, Ralph Koltai, Timothy O'Brien, Julia Trevelyan Oman, John Gunter, Alison Chitty, and many others. Should a director be a designer? No more than he should be an actor. A director must *understand* the process of design, and if he is very lucky, he will have the talent to design productions himself – as Komisarjevsky did, and Peter Brook does. A director's job is to get the best out of the designer, just as it is to get the best out of the actors. A designer has to be open to this process; he should not produce what he thinks the director *should* have before they have seen together what they can find. In my experience, the greater the designer, the more open he is to experiment and risk.

Admittedly, the really great stage designer is a rarity. He is not usually a painter, though he may paint; he is rarely a sculptor, though he may sculpt. He is a magician of the theatre, defining space, delighting in texture, and shedding light not on his own interpretation of the play, but on the interpretation created by the whole group, led by the director. And his work must be in balance with the whole. He must support, not embellish; if he draws too much attention to himself, he will be told that he has over-designed, over-decorated. This is a common charge in

1 All European theatre design has developed from the great Greek amphitheatres. This is the Herodes Atticus in Athens, built in AD 161 by the Romans just below the Parthenon. On stage, in 1985, is the National Theatre of Great Britain's production of *Coriolanus*, directed by Peter Hall and designed by JOHN BURY

Photograph by Peter Hall

Britain, because British puritanism is still to some extent against 'shows'. Inigo Jones was the first great British stage designer, yet even now there are still academics in this country who regard his wonderful court masques as decadent, because the words became, if not superfluous, then certainly subordinate. The British have constant illusions of purity and restraint about stage design, but they combine these with outbreaks of immoderate spectacle, like a reformed drunkard going on a binge. From the spectacular excesses of Victorian melodrama to those of *Phantom of the Opera* or *Starlight Express* today, British design is always teetering dangerously on the edge of a dazzling style with little content. Perhaps that is what makes our designers so superb?

With this puritanism goes an understandable distrust of stage machinery – or spaces which revolve or slide or turn or somersault. For whatever a stage does, it must be silent; however it moves, it must be effortless. Now that everything is technically possible, it is salutary to go to Drottningholm in Sweden to see the purity and simplicity of Baroque theatre. Every cloth, every piece of sliding scenery, every turning *periactoi*, is connected to a central understage capstan: when it moves everything moves, and when it stops everything stops. No computer could do better.

But in being wary of stage machinery designers are brought back to the heart of the matter, which is to recognize that the theatre loves and needs ambiguity. The machine must not be the thing itself but a metaphor, like the Baroque gods flying down from the heavens on a painted cloud, or Mother Courage tramping round her revolving stage as she pulls her cart through the Thirty Years' War. Absolute reality in the theatre is so crude and palpable that it is ridiculous and can make us laugh. A dog on the stage is distracting because he is no more than a dog. He is so obvious that he is comic. We would find the same, I am sure, if we saw an express train rush across the stage as it did in the great days of Drury Lane melodrama. Now that the screen has taken over the expression of naturalism, the stage is even more a place of imaginative make-believe. The camera puts light through celluloid and gives us pictures which we accept as reality. But the theatre puts one or two objects on a planked wooden floor, throws light on them, and asks the audience to believe they are seeing, let us say, ancient Rome. If the choices of the designer are neither archaeologically oppressive, nor inappropriate, the audience will joyfully play this game of make-believe and a whole society will be created for the play.

Great stage design is visionary. The work of Adolphe Appia, Gordon Craig, and Caspar Neher opened up worlds which our great British designers are still exploring. It is a world of space and of lightness; of suggestion rather than actuality; of eclecticism rather than period accuracy. But, unlike the painter, the designer cannot say it all alone. His most powerful collaborators are the actor and the text. He must make the world and the suit of clothes in which the actor can live, be understood, and work on our emotions. Together they express the play.

The author was director of Britain's National Theatre from 1973 to 1988, succeeding Laurence Olivier. He created the Royal Shakespeare Company in 1960 and was its director until 1968. Knighted in 1977, he has directed over 140 productions: modern plays, classics, and operas; also a number of films.

THE YEARS BEFORE

ROY STRONG

As for everything else, peace in 1945 meant for British theatre design not a new beginning but a picking up of the threads so rudely broken in 1939. This is neatly summed up in two of the most scenically famous productions of the immediate post-war period: Cecil Beaton's *Lady Windermere's Fan* at the Haymarket Theatre in 1945 and Oliver Messel's *Sleeping Beauty* with which the Royal Opera House was re-opened the following year. Both designers were already well established in the 1930s and both epitomized the state of theatre design in this country at that period.

Messel and Beaton were the first British designers to lift the status of the profession in the public eye. This was due not so much to their innate talent but to their social background. Messel was the son of Colonel Leonard Messel of Nymans, a huge country house in Sussex. His sister, Anne, was Countess of Rosse and his nephew was the future Lord Snowdon. Beaton had less distinguished antecedents but he had established himself, by sheer force of personality and personal style, at the heart of fashionable society. A production by either of them was news within *le monde* and it would be true to say that no designers since have occupied quite such a position. Both were fundamentally exponents of British insularity, firm adherents to that between-the-wars neo-romanticism which had so firmly rejected the modernist movement and whose most famous exponent was Rex Whistler. Both approached the stage in painterly terms, in those of cloths and cut cloths and flats arranged to create pictures bound by a frame. Messel's *Sleeping Beauty* had the transparency of a watercolour by Turner – washes of pale blue, grey and green with occasional

flickers of gold – strong colour being reserved for details in the costumes. Enchantment was the key-note, reflected in the fact that Messel preferred to be credited as having 'decorated' a production rather than having designed it. So too was it for Beaton who swept his audiences away into a *beau monde* of high glamour and chic bearing no relation to the reality of Wilde's play; instead he presented them – in a grey era of austerity – with a never-never land of security before the devastation of two world wars and the dissolution of the old class system.

Both designers had been used by Ninette de Valois, Robert Helpmann and Frederick Ashton in the company that was to become the Royal Ballet. This company sprang directly out of the Diaghilev tradition, the most innovative force in theatre design during the first half of the century. Avant garde painters, such as Picasso and Matisse, were asked to provide scenery and costumes, and this it was that must have inspired its English counterpart to look for modern British painters who could work in the theatre. Of these, two were to be major forces in the post-war period. The first was John Piper whose earliest important work was a ballet called *The Quest* (1943), and who was to go on to design all Benjamin Britten's operas, beginning with *Albert Herring* in 1947 and ending, almost thirty years later, with *Death in Venice* in 1973. When Piper began to work in theatre he was at the forefront of the modern movement in Britain, responding to the art of Miró, Braque and Picasso but with all dangerous possibilities removed as though transmuted by the eyes of Tudor England. The other artist was Leslie Hurry, whose first production was *Swan Lake* in 1942, one which, in various re-worked versions, was to remain in the Royal Ballet's repertoire until the 1980s when it was replaced by a new production with Yolanda Sonnabend's designs. Hurry's work was very different from that of Piper's, a rare British response to surrealism, the stage being a vehicle for fantastic, hallucinatory visions, restless, tortured and introspective, but with a brilliance which still remains largely unrecognized. Hurry became virtually a full-time designer; he produced his most famous work in the Forties and Fifties, in particular the barbaric *Turandot* at Covent Garden in 1947 and the long series of productions at the Old Vic stretching from 1944 to the early Sixties, including *Hamlet* (1944) and *Tamburlaine* (1951).

To this galaxy I would add a third, Tanya Moiseiwitsch, who did not work for the opera or ballet, but who was prolific at the Old Vic during the Tyrone

2 Edwardian make-believe: **Lady Windermere's Fan**, designed by CECIL BEATON (Theatre Royal, Haymarket, 1945).

Production photograph by Cecil Beaton courtesy of Sotheby's, London

Guthrie period virtually as resident designer. Later she went on to design at Stratford-upon-Avon. With Guthrie she pioneered new ways of staging Shakespeare with the earliest mobile architectural sets I can remember, which greatly speeded the action.

These designers were to be the victims of a cruel fate, all of them going out of fashion at the opening of the 1960s as a result of a revolution in theatre. Oliver Messel left England permanently for Barbados and turned to architecture; Leslie Hurry found work abroad at Stratford, Ontario, as did Tanya Moiseiwitsch; Piper returned to painting, except when called upon by Britten; and Beaton, with the major exception of his costumes for *My Fair Lady*, returned to photography.

The painterly tradition did not die, however; rather it took a new direction in the 1960s responding to the *verismo* style of Franco Zeffirelli and Lila de Nobili. This took on board the change in perception generated in the public by both film and, by 1960, television, which made any stage experience flimsy in comparison. The new lightweight construction materials permitted a new realism on stage: sets were elaborately built and there was a huge multiplication of props. The *verismo* style looked back to the nineteenth century in its desire to re-create gigantic stage pictures – breathtaking in concept, but still bound by the optical rules of single-point perspective. It was a style particularly suited to the great war-horses of opera and ballet, but it was not one which produced any recognizable 'school' in this country, apart from de Nobili's protégé, Henry Bardon, and more particularly one especial talent, Julia Trevelyan Oman. Her relatively few productions, opening with the unforgettable set for Aubrey's *Brief Lives* (1968), are savoured as collector's items.

The main thrust in theatre design after 1960 was to be very different. It was affected by a new generation of directors, above all by Peter Hall and Trevor Nunn; by new theatres, such as Chichester, which are open, arena stages; by the advent of stage design as an academic discipline within the colleges of art; and by huge advances in technology, above all in the emergence of lighting expertise which could literally make or break a production. The new approach was

3

certainly not painterly, nor over-concerned with historical exactitude or detail. Its focus lay in achieving that dramatic celerity familiar to audiences used to film and television. Nothing was either to impede action, the development of dramatic tension, or to detract from the centrality of the text, or divide audience and actors from a shared experience. The theatre ceased to be an escape from the dreariness of post-war Britain into a magic world; rather, in the 1960s and 1970s, it was theatre which reminded its audiences – buoyant in the 'You never had it so good' era – that an unpleasant real world still existed. Black

3 Faerie grandeur:
The Sleeping Beauty,
designed by OLIVER
MESSEL (Sadler's Wells
Ballet, 1946).

*Production photograph by Frank
Sharman*

and grey predominated and whole theatres and sets became monuments to a Stygian gloom.

The inspiration for this new wave came from the work of Karl von Appen for the Berliner Ensemble. However, the first designer to overwhelm the public with this new dynamism and vision was Sean Kenny, whose background was in architecture and not painting and who came out of the left-wing stable of Joan Littlewood. Tragically, he died young but no one who saw his designs for the musical *Oliver!* (1960) will ever forget the huge impact of those vast moving constructions on stage which were quite thrilling to

4

his work at Glyndebourne – also with Hall – was Bury allowed a glimmer of what we know as a designer's curtain, both in the ravishing, glittering, moving wood in Britten's *A Midsummer Night's Dream* (1981) and in the astounding aerial machinery for *La Calisto* (1970) and also *Il Ritorno d'Ulisse in Patria* (1972). Ironically these productions contained the seeds from which was to spring the theatre of mechanical marvels in the late 1970s and 1980s – musicals like *Evita* (1978) and *Phantom of the Opera* (1986).

Within that genre no one could assail that duo, although other important designers did contribute – among them Timothy O'Brien, Jocelyn Herbert and Ralph Koltai – but they were working out aspects of a revolution rather than making one.

In spite of the fact that theatre design as we know it today sprang out of a rejection of the painterly tradition, there is a deeply held, if misguided belief, that somehow movements in contemporary painting should be put on stage. For some mysterious reason it is a view fervently expounded by the Arts Council; also one adopted by the Royal Opera House, who appointed the critic, Bryan Robertson, to seek out such artists in what seems a throwback to the 1940s.

watch. Overnight they rendered the post-war painterly vision not only obsolete but effete. Nothing was to be quite the same again, as these innovations were taken up, modified and expanded by a whole generation of designers – headed by John Bury, whose alliance with Peter Hall was to dominate the British stage for two decades. Bury came from the same left-wing stable as Kenny, and entered theatre design entirely uncluttered by any preconceptions. His working methods epitomized the shift, for he worked entirely through the use of models; having no art school training, he was virtually unable to draw, as indeed his costume designs reveal. This abandonment of the painterly tradition made him the ideal vehicle for Hall, whose rejection of the old means of illusion (except when they suited him) was also total; he wanted a designer who would never usurp either text or actors or director and in Bury he got his man. Their collaboration is now theatrical history. In many ways it was the theatre of the word reborn, and only in

4 Surrealist fantasy: **Swan Lake**, designed by LESLIE HURRY; on the Queen's right is Robert Helpmann as Siegfried (Sadler's Wells Ballet, 1943).

Theatre Museum, courtesy of the Board of Trustees of the Victoria and Albert Museum

5 Gothic abstract: **The Quest**, designed by JOHN PIPER; Robert Helpmann, centre, as the Red Cross Knight (Sadler's Wells Ballet, 1943).

Theatre Museum, courtesy of the Board of Trustees of the Victoria and Albert Museum

5

This explains why what happens on the stage at Covent Garden is so different from what happens elsewhere. No other opera house, ballet company or theatre pursues it (apart from Rambert), preferring instead to work with professional designers who are fully experienced in the arduous techniques of theatre.

On the whole the results have been mixed, and occasionally catastrophic; one recalls Christopher Lebrun's disastrous *Ballet Imperial* (1985) amongst others. But in the 1960s and 1970s this policy did produce one great international designer, in fact the only one that this country has produced since the war, the Greek-born Nicholas Georgiadis. From 1955 onwards he enjoyed a long collaboration with the choreographer, Kenneth MacMillan, but his masterpieces were later: *Romeo and Juliet* (1965), *Manon* (1974) and *Mayerling* (1978). He was also to design some of the great classics: *The Sleeping Beauty* (Milan, 1966, re-staged for the Festival Ballet, 1975), *The Nutcracker* (Royal Ballet, 1967, re-staged Milan 1969) and *Swan Lake* (Vienna, 1964). Georgiadis assimilated the new techniques of scenic change. He made them work in the service of a re-invigorated painterly tradition in which set succeeds set in a mosaic of abstract colour and with a splendour of quite unsurpassed brilliance. He was to influence a whole new generation of designers, among them Yolanda Sonnabend and Stefanos Lazaridis.

No account of the 1970s would be complete, however, without reference to David Hockney, who worked first for the theatre in 1975 with his now celebrated series of designs for *The Rake's Progress* (1975), followed three years later by *The Magic Flute*. Although these have thrilled audiences because of the artist's quite magical power to delight, as theatre design they are remembered more for their great technical shortcomings – from the length of time needed to change the sets to an inability to light the flat painted cloths. Hockney's work is a throwback to the Diaghilev era and it is difficult to place it within the mainstream of theatre design in the last fifty years. Nonetheless, as with the work of all great artists, Hockney's designs will have an immortality beyond those by more proficient designers, and the fact that they fell short on stage will be forgotten.

6

6 Costume designs by LESLIE HURRY for the Chamberlain, the Drummer Boy, and Lear's Pages in **King Lear**; John Gielgud played Lear, and also directed the play with Anthony Quayle (Stratford-upon-Avon, 1950).

(Private collection)

In 1973, with the oil crisis, Britain and the rest of Western Europe entered the long years of economic recession, ones which profoundly affected the cultural ethos. These were the years leading up to the Thatcher revolution, which can now so easily be seen as the end of an epoch, the finale of a vision of the arts as the manifestation of a beneficent state. Roaring inflation radically curtailed theatre budgets and the era of cuts dawned. In the case of theatre, who was the first to be lampooned for reckless extravagance at the taxpayers' expense? Not the producer, nor the director, nor the actors or the technical and stage staff. Ironically, it was to be that poorly paid, overworked and under-appreciated artist, the designer.

The author – writer, historian, broadcaster, and creator of exhibitions – was director of the Victoria and Albert Museum from 1974 to 1987, director of the National Portrait Gallery from 1967 to 1973, and chairman of the Arts Council Arts Panel from 1983 to 1987. He was knighted in 1982.

PLAYS

Michael Ratcliffe

During the course of the 1980s British classical theatre moved from leather to garbage, towards conspicuous consumption, architectural grandeur and a kind of magpie, eclectic resourcefulness whereby actors wore whatever their characters might most appropriately have worn had they been around at this time. The Eighties ended in a vertiginous disorientation stemming both from German Expressionism in the Twenties and from Russian Constructivism before and after 1917.

Years of increased prosperity for the bulk of the theatre-going classes have stimulated a theatre of spectacle, delight and pictorial indulgence, tempered and darkened along the way by historically more sophisticated designers like Ralph Koltai, Jocelyn Herbert, Alison Chitty, Timothy O'Brien and Philip Prowse. As the illusion of spiritual fitness is chipped away, however, younger designers are creating environments in which nothing is certain and you can no longer be sure of the ground under your own feet. Not even gravity has survived intact.

Designers' Theatre has become an unthinking term of abuse used by frustrated writers and actors, and certainly the Eighties have confirmed the rise of the designer as star, most prominently John Napier (*Nicholas Nickleby*), William Dudley (*The Mysteries*) and John Gunter (*Guys and Dolls*). All of them, while hardly household names, pull in a large public by the theatrical power and spectacular beauty of their work.

The widespread misunderstanding of what designers are actually supposed/allowed to do continues, however, as does the compulsion of West End audiences to clap any set which offers as perfect and jam-packed a replica as possible of what they would like their homes to be. The applause is particularly warm if escape is offered for two or three hours to an earlier, more sensitive time. Europe differs in kind but not in degree: France being at heart a bucolic nation,

7

7 **The Oresteia**. Aeschylus, version Tony Harrison

DESIGNER JOCELYN HERBERT. Chorus of Trojan Women (men in women's masks).

National Theatre (Olivier), 1981
Director Peter Hall
Lighting John Bury
Production photograph by Nobby Clark

Parisians are turned on by the dark clash of civilization and nature (Richard Peduzzi, designing for Patrice Chéreau in Marivaux's *La dispute*) or the full working reproduction of a seventeenth-century barn (Ezio Frigerio, for Roger Planchon in Molière's *L'avare*). In urban Germany and Britain it is still more likely to be a large, middle-class sitting-room of the last hundred years with south-facing windows (Lucio Fanti, for *Three Sisters* in Berlin). Both Fanti and Frigerio had worked in Britain by the end of the Eighties, and it is hard to believe that the extraordinary *Dispute*, execrated on its visit to the South Bank in 1976, would have been received so fiercely ten years later. Things are changing here.

The designer, like the writer and director, may flatter or disturb the dreams of the spectators. We in Britain are famously wary of the irrational and the surreal, of the hurricane outside the window or the beast beneath the stairs. No dragon is likely to cross the desert floor of a mainstream stage in this country while men and women go about their business (Robert Wilson's *Alcestis*, Cambridge, Mass., 1986); no lovestruck spinster will wade waist-deep and fully clothed through a deep pool for love of a young man (Karl-Ernst Herrmann for Luc Bondy's production of Marivaux's *Triumph of Love*, Berlin, 1986); by the same token there is unlikely to be an extra half-hour interval while the pool is being drained. Yet design as an agent of disruption flourishes at theatres in Glasgow, Edinburgh, Sheffield and Leicester and among smaller touring groups like Actors Touring Company, Shared Experience and Cheek by Jowl. They, like the opera companies in Leeds, Cardiff, and at the London Coliseum, are connected to Europe direct, taking more risks than either the National or the RSC.

Metropolitan theatre companies have certainly been less willing to risk the new allusive minimalism of designers like Tom Cairns and Antony McDonald who have been designing Shakespeare, Ibsen, Chekhov, Schiller and Tennessee Williams with a bracing, offhand asymmetry, graffiti and grubby white paper walls, sometimes combined with painted perspectives and landscapes of High Victorian skill. In a Sheffield Crucible *Streetcar Named Desire*, Blanche Dubois walked on to a tiny piazza, like Carroll's Alice, an actress in a play of her own dreaming (McDonald); a majestic Norwegian fjord covered one entire studio wall for a Glasgow Citizens *Lady from the Sea* (Cairns). Cairns also designed the Surrealist hangover-dream of the Crucible *Twelfth Night* in which Feste set fire to a dead Christmas tree and plunged it, spitting and crackling, into a stream at the front of the stage. Slowly the flames died out, his final song was done, blackness and silence descended as the play ended.

This poetic theatre of watchers and dreamers, mystery and threat, probing the audience's collective subconscious and reminding them of things they had forgotten they ever knew, almost certainly derives from Chéreau's production of Wagner's *Ring* cycle at Bayreuth (1976–80). Chéreau's influence, preserved on video and in books, continues to spread like ripples across a pool, not least among designers and directors who have never sat through a Wagner opera.

The designer who has absorbed and practised its lessons most inventively in British theatre – though he himself is Irish – is Bob Crowley, whose partnership with the director Adrian Noble has produced some of the most original work in an often disappointing decade on the main RSC stage at Stratford-upon-Avon: *Measure for Measure*, *Henry V*, *As You Like It* and *The Plantagenets*. These two have worked with equal success in small spaces: their 1984 *The Winter's Tale* was a promenade touring production played in clothes which alluded, without declaring the affinity directly, to the lost world of the early 1950s: Paulina was a small, febrile woman with cropped hair like Judy Garland; the Sicilian Court combined the innocent artificiality of the young English royals with the bandit Giuliano's *mafiosi*; the messengers returned from Delphi like displaced persons still travelling years after the end of the Second World War. The forgotten iconography of the recent past is peculiarly poignant, and this *Winter's Tale* – memory and disorientation play important parts in Shakespeare's play – drew on it with subtlety and direct, emotional force, the Fifties marking the adolescence and early adulthood of middle-aged theatre-goers.

Indeed, under the mysterious, unwritten thirty-year rule which governs the tribal memory, the later

Forties and early Fifties have come into hard focus for the first time in recent years: it was the last age before the present in which women were forced into stiff frocks for the amusement of men, an age whose fatuous innocence and complacency have not been questioned seriously until now. Not too seriously, though: Bill Dudley set the RSC's 1985 *Merry Wives of Windsor* in the wizard-prang world and 'New Elizabethanism' of Battle of Britain pilots, Ealing comedy, toreador pants and suburban young men trying to look 'Beat', and the parallel fitted Shakespeare's *nouveau riche* farce to perfection. In *Kiss Me Kate*, for the RSC two years later, he revelled in the early Fifties once more, even daring affectionate jokes about the original New York designs.

More usefully, recent history has aided the discovery that Racine – supposedly unstageable outside the corset of French Alexandrine verse – was an intimate chamber dramatist with timeless things to say about love and politics, public and private life: a modern-dress *Bérénice* (Lyric Studio, 1982) was followed by Cheek by Jowl's *Andromache* (1985), in which Nick Ormerod brilliantly transposed the action from the aftermath of the Trojan War to the bitter recriminations of post-war France. The American office and small-town paintings of Edward Hopper joined Hollywood movies in the stream of design references for the Forties and Fifties so that gradually sirens with full lips and shoulder-length hair and men in business suits became almost as big an updating cliché as Caroline, Regency and Edwardian dress.

The next time we saw *Andromache*, however, it was on a big stage, with a large, intricate setting that looked as though a bomb had hit it. It was designed by Richard Hudson who, along with Mark Thompson, must be the most idiosyncratic newcomer to establish himself in recent years, and who was also Jonathan Miller's resident designer for his first, 1988, season at the Old Vic. Hudson is the new architect of gravitational riot. His actors played out their drama in a classical saloon vertiginously tilted to the right inside the shell of a baroque hall: the duality of Racine's art made manifest. The roof of the suburban home in *One Way Pendulum* was blown clean off, to expose the logic and battiness of the inhabitants to a bright blue cuckooland sky. In Ostrovsky's *Too Clever By Half* gasping petitioners heaved themselves breathlessly into the scoundrel's apartment as though two steps were missing at the top of the unseen stairs; the canny clung to the walls thereafter for fear of being sucked into the centre of the room. A large Christian cross exploded in fire at the start of *Don Carlos* (Royal Exchange Theatre, Manchester, 1987). Hudson's world is a very unsafe place.

Three large new theatres have greatly influenced the course of British design in recent years: Manchester's Exchange and the National's Olivier (both opening in 1976), joined by the Barbican in 1982. The Exchange is galleried and more or less round; the Olivier is an open arena stage, modelled on Epidaurus; the Barbican one might call a proscenium open stage. Two things have happened as consequences of their popularity. A certain gigantism is now almost taken for granted by the public, and it has become harder than ever to be drawn visually and imaginatively into shows on a conventional proscenium stage. The continuing vitality of pub and studio theatre has only compounded the problem.

Big theatres have to be filled with people and most people like their scenery big: the Barbican favoured a handsome sequence of conservatories (*All's Well That Ends Well*, *Misalliance*) and great trees (*Much Ado About Nothing*, *Twelfth Night*, *Cyrano de Bergerac*, *Penny for a Song*); the Olivier a reconstruction of Georgian Bath (*The Rivals*), an impressionistic pre-war Vienna (*Tales from the Vienna Woods*) and an Alpine resort hotel complete with working lift (*Undiscovered Country*). Meticulous architectural settings arrived in the non-lyric theatre for perhaps the first time: at the Olivier the austere and monumental classicism of John Bury for the textual theatre of Peter Hall; at the Barbican a late fourteenth-century garden for *Richard II* (1986), into which the King was placed like a poet in a Book of Hours; a vault of Perpendicular royal tombs for *Richard III* (RSC, 1984); and a large chunk of white Greek island for *Twelfth Night* (RSC, 1987), of which the actors appeared unaware. Few directors and designers risk playing the Barbican stage bare, and even these designs proved harder to use theatrically than to erect: they either inhibited, or had little to do with, the production's vision.

Size, however, does not preclude sharp focus. This was apparent when the curtain rose on Ezio Frigerio's ravine-like Andalusian courtyard for *The House of Bernarda Alba* (Lyric, Hammersmith, 1986). Frigerio is the European master of architectural theatre and draws on a tradition going back to the court spectacles of the Italian Renaissance. For Lorca he designed a secretive, towering sorority hidden from the blinding heat and sun, in which it was possible to choreograph and animate the narrative of the play. Mark Thompson's gigantic marble columns in an RSC *Measure for Measure* (1987) harked back to the Chéreau–Peduzzi *Ring* as they turned to reveal rotting pipes and service-ducts, the obverse of pomposity, the guts of the gilded city corrupt to its municipal heart. The play flourished around them.

Thompson, potentially the next designer with a star's pulling-power, is one of the few since Osbert Lancaster both to make consistently witty, wearable clothes, and to loosen the chastity belt of the Chichester stage (*The Scarlet Pimpernel*), an artist whose fizzy delight in colour and energy matches, at best, the colour, fizz and energy of the play. He can go wrong; he smothered a *Much Ado About Nothing* for the RSC in 1988. But his Royal Exchange *Country Wife*, which drew on five hundred years of English costume from wimples to punk, had little to do with the letter and everything to do with the spirit of Restoration London; the actors gloried in it. If a plain green door on a dark grey wall is all that is required (*The Sneeze*, 1988) he makes something articulate of that, too.

On the South Bank, the National's two larger houses have changed places. Around 1980, the proscenium Lyttelton was going from success to success, while the search for a new heroic style of production and design for the Olivier continued in vain. Now the Olivier is more or less conquered, or at least understood, but the Lyttelton is jinxed with a chilling auditorium and a stage of excessive dimensions, with the reputation for swallowing plays whole. Large sets are not the answer here, and reforms are mooted for the auditorium itself, to revive the lost kinship between audience and stage. (The studio Cottesloe remains the favourite of actors, critics and directors alike.)

8

8   The Country Wife.
Wycherley

DESIGNER MARK THOMPSON. Costume designs for Lady Fidget, Mrs Dainty, Miss Squeamish.

Royal Exchange Theatre, Manchester, 1986
Director Nicholas Hytner
Lighting Paul Pyant

Two shows cracked the Olivier: *The Oresteia* and *Guys and Dolls*. For Aeschylus, Jocelyn Herbert emptied and tiered the stage, intensifying the drama on characters wearing timeless, powerful masks. The actors themselves became a kind of scenery as they did also in the RSC *Nicholas Nickleby* and Shared Experience shows before that. For Frank Loesser and Damon Runyon, John Gunter did the reverse, scribbling all over the sides and back of the stage with working neon advertisements of late Forties' New York. The Olivier was liberated as never before.

The problems remain: Gunter's spectacular *Government Inspector*, like his Barbican *Mephisto*, diminished both performers and play. Dudley, who got the Olivier revolve working for the first time in 1988 in *The Shaughraun* – filling it with a whole coastline of corny Ould Ireland, rising, sinking and turning – almost pushed the actors off the stage five months later in *Bartholomew Fair* with stalls, roundabouts and a mechanical organ. John Napier did the same to

Mother Courage in 1984 at the Barbican, with a single, central device whose ponderous functioning dominated the performance. It is at moments like these that mutterings of Designers' Theatre afflict even those who believe that the importance of design cannot be overstated – as regards both the appearance and interpretation of a play. That said, designers are still too frequently blamed for what is a lack of imagination in lazy directors who have no idea how to inhabit a dynamic design.

The rediscovery of perspective by designers like Hudson suggests a proscenium revival is likely. Philip Prowse remains our only master of the form, both as designer and director, drawing the audience's eye into dramatically three-dimensional settings that are allusive, dangerous, witty and disturbing. There is always more to them than meets the eye, but what meets the eye is rich enough. Most of his work with plays has been at the Glasgow Citizens where he is never outfaced by one of the most flamboyant auditoriums in Britain, and where the lighting – usually by Gerry Jenkinson – is crucial in sustaining an illusion of reality and splendour through plays like *The Vortex*, *Anna Karenina* and *Lady Windermere's Fan*. Like many designers today, Prowse has learned to ignore Shaw's meticulous stage directions, in order to prise out the closet-Symbolist beneath. Over his *Heartbreak House* (1985) hung a huge tree of scarlet flowers; the sky above Shotover's Sussex was raining Flanders blood. For his West End *Phaedra* (1984) the horse and chariot killing Hippolytus crashed through an apparently solid wall to land in a heap at the front of the stage. Only one actor – the veteran Robert Eddison – survived the competition intact.

Is design taking over? Not at all. Much of the time it is not nearly radical enough. British directors and designers alike remain cautious about altering the shape of the audience and the space of the stage. The flexibility of the Cottesloe and The Pit is very underexploited. Lucio Fanti's reduction and expansion of conventional stage openings in Peter Stein's Schaubühne production of *The Hairy Ape* – constructing a vertical staircase the full depth of the proscenium side, and stacking the decks of the ship in hierarchic rectangles from top to bottom of the stage –

9 **Cymbeline**. Shakespeare

DESIGNER STEPHEN McCABE. Costume design for Roman captain in battle.

Royal Exchange Theatre, Manchester, 1984
Directors Braham Murray, Gregory Hersov, James Maxwell, Casper Wrede
Lighting Michael Williams

9

was a revelation on its visit to the National in 1987. Its influence was felt almost immediately in McDonald's *Billy Budd* at the ENO and Dudley's sumptuous *Changeling* at the Lyttelton.

Still less do our designers experiment with partial visibility, while visiting companies from Poland (Andrej Wajda's *Crime and Punishment*, 1986) and the Soviet Union (Anatoly Vasiliev's *Cerceau*, 1987) both invited the eye and mind of the audience to imitate the tracking of a camera, imagining through doors, windows and walls what they could not, for the moment, see. Nancy Meckler and The People Show did take the action of *Macbeth* (Leicester Haymarket, 1985) invisibly beneath the floor of the palace at various points to create an environment in which wild and unidentifiable sounds were not only battling through the night air but through the earth as well; and the New Orleans apartment in McDonald's *Streetcar* was bisected transversely across the Crucible thrust-stage by a red net curtain. But we still hold a very restrictive view of the Restricted View.

RSC designers have been slow to make use of the middle air in front of gallery spectators in the new Swan. One exception is (again) Crowley, whose Machevil pierced the floor of the Mediterranean like a rocket on a column of dark ash in *The Jew of Malta*. Marlowe demands a certain bravura. As with the middle air, so with the floor. I would not recommend the experience whereby the theatre of Scipion Nasica from Ljubliana blindfolded Edinburgh audiences and sat them under the stage with their heads sticking out like skittles (1986), but few British designers have animated a stage floor with the imagination of, say, Fanti in *Melancholy Jacques* (Traverse and Bush, 1984). For this one-man play about Rousseau he placed the author of *The Social Contract* on a tiny Swiss island littered with piles of books which, on being opened, released great beams of light into the sky – a powerful and ironic comment on the Age of Enlightenment and on the unquestioning commitment to faith in the written word. It would be hard to pack more historical resonance into so small a space. The floor at the Royal Exchange is both the matrix of the play itself and the equivalent of backcloth or cyclorama to spectators watching the play from

above. In 1984 Stephen McCabe transformed the ground of Cymbeline's Britain into riveted panels of undulating blond wood, which became monuments, refuges and redoubts as the picaresque action required – one of the most moving and seductive images of the entire decade. Ultz set *The Art of Success*, Nick Dear's play about Hogarth, Walpole and the battle against state censorship, on what looked like a trampoline of artist's drawing paper suspended three feet above the floor of the RSC's Other Place. Such a design puts both actors and audience on their keenest mettle to deliver and receive a play.

Some senior directors resist the idea of design which 'tells the story' of a play because they believe it will leave them and their actors with too little to do.

10 **The Marriage**. Gogol, adaptation Mike Alfreds

DESIGNER PAUL DART. Set drawing.

Shared Experience, 1984
Director Mike Alfreds
Lighting Paul Dart

10

Not true, of course. It goes without saying that the three greatest theatrical experiences of recent years – Trevor Nunn and John Caird's *Nicholas Nickleby*, Bill Bryden's *The Mysteries* and, from Paris, Peter Brook's *Mahabharata* cycle – owed their success to a harmony of all the theatrical elements: acting, direction, lighting and design. From ladders, catwalks and the accumulated junk of materialist existence John Napier and Dermot Hayes constructed a magnificent metaphor of urban desolation and resilience that sent the eight-hour Dickensian adventure racing into the four corners of the theatre. Dudley designed a complete environment for the Cottesloe *Mysteries* in which smoky amber light poured down from shining domestic utensils made of punctured tin; God created the firmament from the top of a fork-lift truck; and archangels in the highest gallery beamed the light of faith and retribution down on the upturned faces of the promenading actors and spectators below.

No one will forget *The Mysteries* or *Nicholas Nickleby*. There have, however, been many less ambitious and less expensive triumphs where designers have got potentially difficult projects off to a flying start. Paul Dart's backcloth of chests, wardrobes, clocks and commodes towered like an iconostasis of bourgeois values behind the competing grotesques in the 1984 Mike Alfreds–Shared Experience production of Gogol's *Marriage*. Also in 1984 Voytek contained the five-hour sprawl of O'Neill's *Strange Interlude* inside a dappled clapboard box which matched the perfect East Coast manners with which these over-educated neurotics concealed the violence of their thoughts. A year later he illuminated Strindberg's *Dance of Death* (Riverside) inside a vast membrane of polythene and grey netting which diffused glittering shards of light off the unseen waters of the Stockholm sea.

Sometimes even a single image has captured the essence of a play; the outrageous cocktail cabinet vanishing out of sight in *Summit Conference* (Citizens, then West End, 1983) with which Prowse defined the vulgarity and pretentiousness of the Third Reich; the angel statue of Eternity in the time-stopped Mississippi town square of Williams's *Summer and Smoke* (Dermot Hayes, Leicester Haymarket, 1987); the

11 **California Dog Fight**.
Mark Lee

DESIGNER GRANT HICKS

Bush Theatre, London, 1985
Director Simon Stokes
Lighting Paul Denby
Production photograph by Nicky Pallot
John Shrapnel (Vern)

11

stunted reeds, red scrub and telephone wires stretching to infinity with which Grant Hicks compacted the stifling desert of *California Dog Fight* into the upstairs room at the Bush; above all, the wall of cheap Accrington brick, frozen in mid-collapse, designed by the Canadian Peter Hartwell for Edward Bond's desolate tragedy of working-class ignorance, *Saved* (Royal Court, 1987). Such things remain in the memory long after the argument of a play has gone to ground and the actors' voices have faded away.

The author has been theatre critic of the Observer *since 1984. He was literary editor of* The Times *between 1967 and 1972, and from then until 1982 was its chief book reviewer.*

12A & B **Baal**. Brecht, translation Peter Tegel

DESIGNER RALPH KOLTAI: 'Conceived for a studio theatre with no depth of stage, the three-dimensional wall collage allowed actors easily to remove (and replace) props. The entire surface of the collage was at times "destroyed" by front projections virtually obliterating the basic setting.'

Royal Shakespeare Company (The Other Place), 1979
Director David Jones
Lighting Leo Leibovici
Set photographs by Ralph Koltai

12B

13

13 **Troilus and Cressida**. Shakespeare

SET DESIGNER RALPH KOLTAI: 'The production was set in the mid 19th century, the location intentionally ambiguous: a manor house realistic in impression but not actually so, under siege by Trojans or Greeks alternately.'

Royal Shakespeare Company, 1985
Director Howard Davies
Costume designer Liz da Costa
Lighting Jeffrey Beecroft with Clive Morris
Model photograph by Ralph Koltai

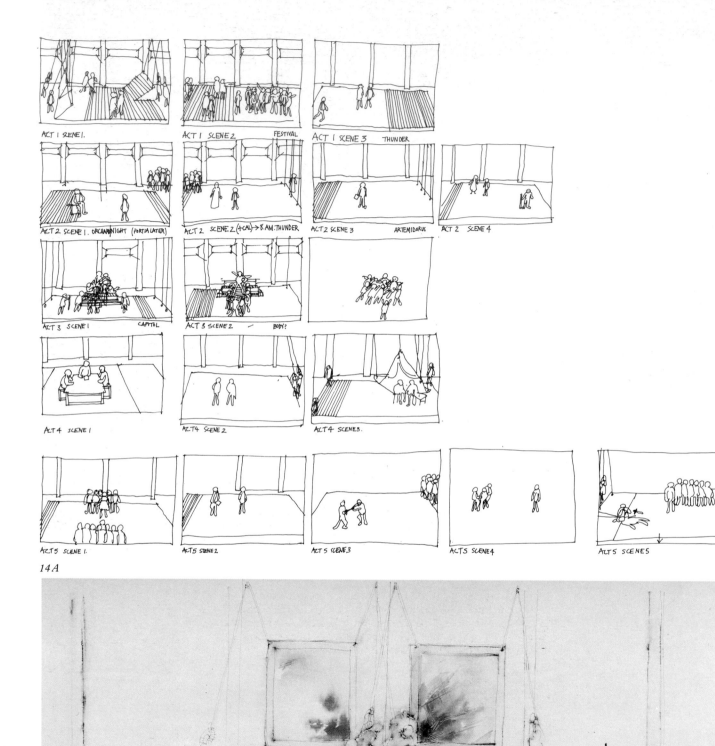

ACT 1 SCENE 1.

ACT 1 SCENE 2.   FESTIVAL

ACT 1 SCENE 3   THUNDER

ACT 2 SCENE 1. ORCHARD NIGHT (PORTIA LATER)

ACT 2 SCENE 2 (+CAL) → 8.AM.THUNDER

ACT 2 SCENE 3   ARTEMIDORUS

ACT 2 SCENE 4

ACT 3 SCENE 1   CAPITOL

ACT 3 SCENE 2   BODY?

ACT 4 SCENE 1

ACT 4 SCENE 2

ACT 4 SCENE 3.

ACT 5 SCENE 1.

ACT 5 SCENE 2.

ACT 5 SCENE 3.

ACT 5 SCENE 4

ACT 5 SCENE 5

14A

14B

14A & B **Julius Caesar**. Shakespeare

DESIGNER ALISON CHITTY: 'In a storyboard (*14A*) I draw the key moments of each scene, which shows me the shape and structure of the play, and where the actors need to be, so that I can design a space to hold them. It's what I call designing from the inside out – not from the outside in.'

'The assassination of Caesar (*14B*) – one of many drawings I made to work out a simple strong style for the production, particularly how to express the violence of the murder and tackle the problem of how to represent blood on stage.'

Riverside Studios, London, 1980
Director Peter Gill
Lighting Rory Dempster

15

15 Martine. Jean-Jacques Bernard, translation John Fowles

DESIGNER ALISON CHITTY: 'The play was performed
without an interval, and the four scene changes had to happen
magically in front of the audience. Act 1, here, is a roadside by a
cornfield in high summer. The corn was made from Chinese
cane window blinds and carpet felt.'

National Theatre (Lyttelton), 1985
Director Peter Hall
Lighting Gerry Jenkinson
Production photograph by John Haynes
Barrie Rutter (Alfred), Wendy Morgan (Martine)

16A & B   **The Late Shakespeares:** Cymbeline, The Winter's Tale, The Tempest. Shakespeare

DESIGNER ALISON CHITTY: 'Suspended above the stage, this representation of a Carolinian view of the heavens (*16A*), the Copernican System, set the plays in the 1620s. It could fly in and out, tilt, open for the gods to fly through, and with light heighten special moments. Miraculously, despite its 1.25 tons, it seemed to float.'

'One of my first drawings for these productions (*16B*). Hidden inside the floor, and the sliding back wall with central doorway, and the roof, was a complicated box of tricks which served all three plays.'

National Theatre (Cottesloe), 1988
Director Peter Hall
Lighting Gerry Jenkinson and Ben Ormerod
Photograph of the heavens by John Haynes

17 **Old Times**. Pinter

DESIGNER TIMOTHY O'BRIEN: 'Harold Pinter's stage directions: "A converted farmhouse. A long window up centre. Bedroom door up left. Front door up right. Spare modern furniture. Two sofas. An armchair. Autumn. Night. Light dim. Three figures discerned."'

Theatre Royal, Haymarket, 1985
Director David Jones
Lighting David Hersey
Production photograph by Timothy O'Brien
Nicola Pagett (Kate), Liv Ullman (Anna), Michael Gambon (Deeley)

17

18 **The American Clock**. Arthur Miller

DESIGNER TIMOTHY O'BRIEN: 'Arthur Miller has called his play a mural, as it deals with memories of the depression, when Americans lived near material despair and survived through dogged faith in their country. The set *was* that mural, abstractly and concretely, and bound the episodes of the story together.'

Set design collage

National Theatre (Cottesloe), 1986
Director Peter Wood
Lighting Robert Bryan

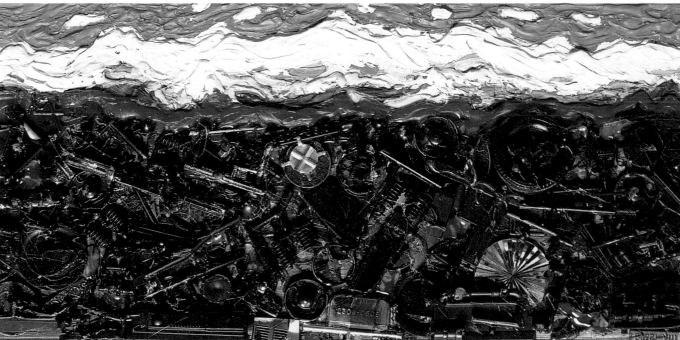

18

19   **Three Sisters**. Chekhov, English version John Barton

SET DESIGNER TIMOTHY O'BRIEN: 'We presented the characters on a chamberscale acting area, but we needed more. The famous yearning of the sisters for Moscow is a pipedream about the past; their call to each other to go on living is about going into a different future and the overcoming of death. For this we set them against a much larger world of nature, of forests and meadows and great distances.'

Royal Shakespeare Company, 1988
Director John Barton
Costumes Louise Belson
Lighting Robert Bryan
Production photograph by Timothy O'Brien
Includes: Harriet Walter (Masha), Brian Cox (Vershinin)

19

20   **The Trojan Women**. Euripides, adaptation Sartre

DESIGNER TAZEENA FIRTH: 'Cassandra: "Darkness would mark my way as I walked towards that bed where I am to be joined to the enemy."'

Stadstheatern, Göteborg, 1986
Director David Radok
Lighting Mauritz de Vries
Production photograph by Ingmar Jernberg
Vanya Blomkvist (Cassandra)

20

PLAYS

21A & B **Once in a Lifetime**. Moss Hart and George
S. Kaufman

DESIGNER JOHN NAPIER: 'A multi-scene romp about
Hollywood in the late Twenties, and the design aimed to reflect
this. I tried for wit and a lightness of touch that was in a sense
akin to a musical. It was enormous fun to do.'

21A The Producer's Office
From left: Carmen du Sautoy (Miss Leighton), Cheryl Hall (Florabel
Leigh), Diana van Fossen (Phyllis Fontaine)

21B Shooting a Wedding on the Sound Stage
Toria Fuller (Susan Walker – bride), Ian Reddington (Cyril Fonsdale –
groom), George Raistrick (Bishop)

Royal Shakespeare Company, 1979
Director Trevor Nunn
Ladies' costumes designed by Andreane Neofitou
Lighting Robert Bryan
Production photographs by Donald Cooper

22 **Henry VI Part 1**. Shakespeare

DESIGNER JOHN NAPIER: 'The Barbican opened with both
parts of *Henry IV*. The stage was new and *big*. Four platforms
carrying different structures crossed and linked in many
permutations to create both intimate domestic scenes and epic
events and battles.'

Royal Shakespeare Company, 1982
Director Trevor Nunn
Lighting David Hersey
Production photograph by Chris Davies
Includes from left: Joss Ackland (Falstaff), Gerard Murphy (Hal), Hugh
Quarshie (Vernon), John Franklyn-Robbins (Worcester), Patrick
Stewart (Henry IV)

21A

21B

22

37

23A

23B

23A & B **Nicholas Nickleby**. Dickens, adaptation
David Edgar

DESIGNER JOHN NAPIER: 'By the time of *Nickleby* Trevor
Nunn and I were totally in tune because of all the other work
we'd done together. What happened on stage here grew from a
long period of improvisation. I wanted the design to embody
Victorian qualities which the actors could make their own.'

Royal Shakespeare Company, 1980
Director Trevor Nunn and John Caird
Co-designer Dermot Hayes
Lighting David Hersey
Model photograph by Chris Davies (23A)
Production photograph by Chris Davies (23B)
Centre: Roger Rees (Nicholas)

24

24 **Animal Farm**. Orwell,
adaptation Peter Hall, lyrics
Adrian Mitchell

DESIGNER JENNIFER
CAREY: 'We searched for an
innocent style. A young
schoolboy narrated. The
animals and humans were
masked; four legs were
achieved with crutches; the
scale of chickens was solved by
wearing the whole animal on
the head. The toy farm
scenery moved, turned, and
opened revealing new parts of
the farm.'

National Theatre (Cottesloe),
1984
Director Peter Hall
Lighting John Bury

25 More Light. Snoo Wilson

DESIGNER ROBIN DON: 'The play demands the creation – in this case on a small stage (13 ft by 21 ft) – of the intense imaginative world of the Renaissance theatre of memory. Objects were manoeuvred around reflective surfaces, conjuring up Heaven, Rome, and a luminous scarab which burned up as it flew into the sun.'

Bush Theatre, London, 1987
Directors Simon Stokes and Snoo Wilson
Lighting Paul Denby
Production photograph by Nobby Clark
Caroline Holdaway (the Barmaid)

26 Mary Stuart. Schiller, translation Robert David MacDonald

DESIGNER ANTONY McDONALD: 'Schiller never intended his play to be a historical re-creation; he was more concerned with politics and personality. In our production Elizabeth is as restricted and confined as Mary. The idea that they could not survive in the same world was the main theme in the design.'

Greenwich Theatre, London, 1988
Director Tim Albery
Lighting Christopher Toulmin
Production photograph by Carol Baugh
From left: Paola Dionisotti (Elizabeth), Lorcan Cranitch (Leicester), Fiona Shaw (Mary Stuart)

26

25

27

27 **Fuente Ovejuna**.
Lope de Vega, version Adrian
Mitchell

DESIGNER NICK ORMEROD:
'The play was staged simply,
in the traverse, against a
painted landscape drop, in the
permanent presence of the
King and Queen. It was a
space of confrontation,
processions, and rituals in
which the audience were
implicated.'

National Theatre (Cottesloe),
1989
Director Declan Donnellan
Lighting Mick Hughes
Production photograph of a group of
villagers by Robert Workman

28 **Pericles**. Shakespeare

DESIGNER NICK ORMEROD:
'The set was an easily
adaptable arena, hung with
musical instruments and
dominated by a representation
of the goddess Diana. Each of
the actors played a number of
parts in identical costumes,
and used a direct and swift
narrative style to tell a story
which moves through many
changes of place and time.'

Cheek by Jowl, 1984
Director Declan Donnellan
Production photograph by Peter
Mareš
From left: Simon Dormandy,
Amanda Harris, Andrew Collins,
Michael Rigg, Duncan Bell

28

29

29 Futurists. Dusty Hughes

DESIGNER WILLIAM DUDLEY: 'The idea of the design was to make palpable the energy of artists that was released immediately after the Russian revolution, a time when anything seemed possible. The setting was physically ripped down by the actors as Stalinism took over.'

National Theatre (Cottesloe), 1986
Director Richard Eyre
Lighting Peter Radmore
Set photograph by Robert Workman

30A

30A & B **The Changeling**. Middleton and Rowley

DESIGNER WILLIAM DUDLEY: 'The design was based on Spanish colonial plantations of the late Goya period. The set and costumes were an expression of that society's structure and fabric. The inner chamber had the gilded face of the polite, moneyed world; the staircases and corridors were inhabited by outsiders – servants, assassins, madmen.'

National Theatre (Lyttelton), 1988
Director Richard Eyre
Lighting Mark Henderson
Production photographs by John Haynes
30A George Harris (De Flores), Linal Haft (Tomazo de Piracquo)
30B Centre: Rebecca Pidgeon (Isabella), Paul Barber (Lollio)

31 **Bartholomew Fair**. Jonson

DESIGNER WILLIAM DUDLEY: 'We updated the action to *c.* 1895: the British and European funfairs at the turn of the century reached a zenith of decorative brilliance whilst retaining an earlier vulgarity and daring. That seemed to express what Jonson was celebrating in the play's gallery of rogues.'

National Theatre (Olivier), 1988
Director Richard Eyre
Lighting David Hersey
Production photograph by John Haynes
From left: Peter-Hugo Daly (hobby-horse seller), Jonathan Cullen (a cutpurse), Guy Henry (Bartholomew Cokes), Jim Barclay (a ballad singer), Maggie McCarthy (Joan Trash), John Wells (Adam Overdo)

32A

32B

32A & B **The Mysteries**: The Nativity, The Passion and Doomsday. Version by the company with Tony Harrison

DESIGNER WILLIAM DUDLEY: 'I had to find an unpatronising modern equivalent to the spiritual certainties of the medieval guild-workers who acted and made the plays. Where, for instance, they used stonemason's techniques to raise God up at the Creation, we used a fork-lift truck; hurricane lamps and dustbin braziers became the firmament(*32A*).'

'We wanted the end of the three-play cycle, Doomsday, to have clear implications – a global nuclear Armageddon (*32B*) – and following our line of naive literalism we showed the condemned skewered in agony on a ferris-wheel, the spinning earth.'

32A The Creation
Brian Glover (God)

32B Doomsday

National Theatre (Cottesloe, promenade production), 1985
Director Bill Bryden
Lighting William Dudley and Laurence Clayton
Production photographs by Nobby Clark (32A) and Donald Cooper (32B)

33

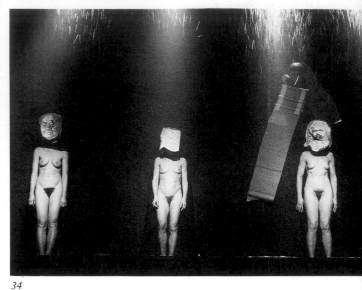

34

33 **Twelfth Night**. Shakespeare

SET DESIGNER KIT SURREY: 'We wanted a sun-bleached Mediterranean environment where the heat has driven all the characters slightly mad. Escher's drawings were a springboard for my ideas, resulting in a maze of steps, roofs and alleyways, reflecting the confusions inherent in the play.'

Royal Shakespeare Company, 1987
Director Bill Alexander
Costume designer Deirdre Clancy
Lighting Robert Bryan
Production photograph by Ivan Kyncl
Deborah Findlay (Olivia), Bruce Alexander (Feste), Harriet Walter (Viola)

34 **Hamletmachine**. Heiner Müller, translation Carl Weber

SET DESIGNER PETER MUMFORD: 'A compressed version of *Hamlet*. Dealing with some of the main themes in the play, it juxtaposed them with ideas and images of this century.'

St Stephen's Theatre Space, Cardiff, 1985
Director (and Lighting) Peter Mumford
Costume designer Candida Cook
Production photograph by Mary Giles
Nude figures: Jenny Baylis, Jessica Cohen, Belinda Neave;
Nick Birkinshaw (Hamlet)

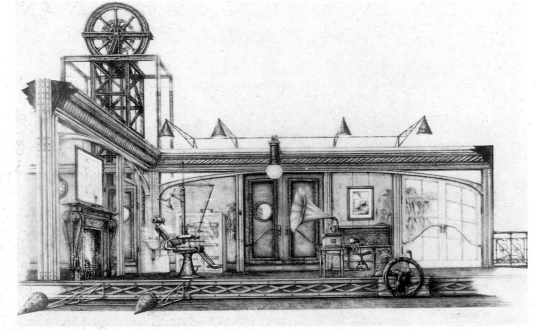

35

35 **Scenes from a Marriage**. Feydeau, adaptation Peter Barnes

DESIGNER GERALD HOWLAND: 'A Parisian apartment at the turn of the century (Act 1). Its mechanically transparent appearance was an image for the manic ferris-wheel activities of the protagonists.'

Royal Shakespeare Company, 1986
Director Terry Hands
Lighting Terry Hands with Clive Morris

37

36 Orders of Obedience

DESIGNER SANDY POWELL: 'A famous 16th-century reference, topped with huge hats inspired by Malcolm Poynter's sculpture, balanced by equally huge skirts. The show, a wacky theatrical ritual, was a Rational Theatre collaboration influenced by, among others, the Japanese Buto company, Sankai Juku.'

Rational Theatre, 1981
Director Andy Wilson
Lighting Ian Gugan
Production photograph by Robyn Beech
Sarah Sankey, Christine Bowler

37 Hiawatha. Longfellow, adaptation Michael Bogdanov

DESIGNER MARTY FLOOD: 'This was a chance to find striking but simple images which allowed the actors to tell and become the story. An enormous skeletal teepee, a huge moon, splashes of Indian design and colours, became Hiawatha's world.'

National Theatre (Olivier), 1980
Director Michael Bogdanov
Lighting Chris Ellis
Production photograph (from play's '81/'82 revival) by Laurence Burns
Stephen Hattersley (the West Wind), Frederick Warder (Hiawatha)

36

38

38 The Park. Botho Strauss, translation Tinch Minter and Anthony Vivis

DESIGNER TOM CAIRNS: 'Oberon and Titania return to earth (i.e. a park in Germany) hoping to discover why the human race has become lost in 20th-century materialism. Everyone in the play lives in or near the park. The photograph shows lovers quarrelling. The trees have crept into the house as the argument explodes into violence.'

Crucible Theatre, Sheffield, 1988
Directors Steven Pimlott and Clare Venables
Lighting Davy Cunningham
Production photograph by Ivan Kyncl
From left: Simon Roberts (Wolf), Miriam Cyr (Helen), Jane Gurnett (Helma), Crispin Redman (George)

39

39 The Winter's Tale. Shakespeare

DESIGNER TOM CAIRNS: 'In contrast to the colour and warmth of the later scenes in Bohemia, the world of Sicilia was empty, cold and desolate. The mountain in this picture slowly descends into the ground as the Sicilian court mourn for the queen and the child King Leontes believes he has lost.'

Crucible Theatre, 1987
Director Steven Pimlott
Lighting Davy Cunningham
Production photograph by Alex von Koettlitz
From left: Robert Patterson (a lord), Jim Broadbent (Leontes)

41

40

40   **Uncle Vanya**. Chekhov, translation Christopher Hampton

DESIGNER TOM CAIRNS: 'The set for this studio production was two large moving walls forming the corner of a room for most of the play. The scene here shows Vanya leaving after attempting to shoot the professor. Yelena, the professor's wife, lies on the floor.'

The Crucible Studio Theatre, Sheffield, 1987
Director Tom Cairns
Lighting Matthew Richardson
Production photograph by Tom Cairns
Matthew Long (Vanya), Helen Cooper (Yelena)

41   **Twelfth Night**. Shakespeare

DESIGNER TOM CAIRNS: 'Sebastian to Olivia (Act 4, Scene 1): "What relish is in this? how runs the stream?/Or am I mad? or else this is a dream./ Let fancy still my sense in Lethe steep;/If it be thus to dream, still let me sleep."'

Crucible Theatre, Sheffield, 1987
Director Steven Pimlott
Lighting Davy Cunningham
Production photograph by Alex von Koettlitz
Helen Cooper (Olivia), Lucien Taylor (Sebastian)

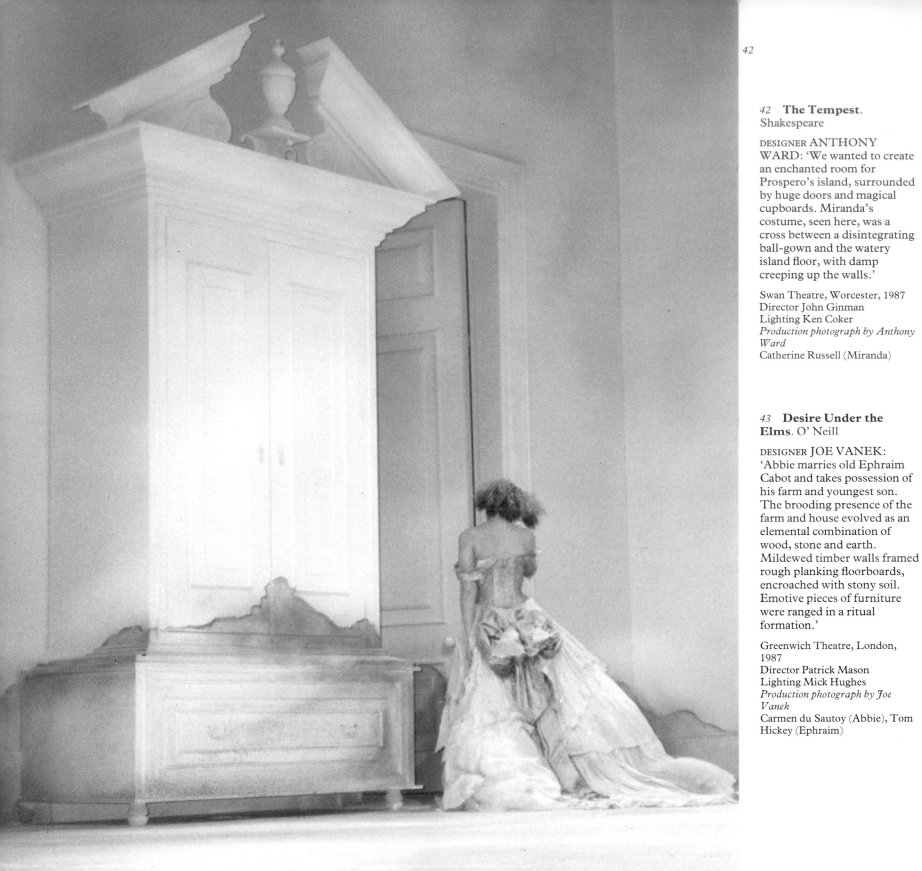

42 **The Tempest**.
Shakespeare

DESIGNER ANTHONY
WARD: 'We wanted to create
an enchanted room for
Prospero's island, surrounded
by huge doors and magical
cupboards. Miranda's
costume, seen here, was a
cross between a disintegrating
ball-gown and the watery
island floor, with damp
creeping up the walls.'

Swan Theatre, Worcester, 1987
Director John Ginman
Lighting Ken Coker
*Production photograph by Anthony
Ward*
Catherine Russell (Miranda)

43 **Desire Under the
Elms**. O' Neill

DESIGNER JOE VANEK:
'Abbie marries old Ephraim
Cabot and takes possession of
his farm and youngest son.
The brooding presence of the
farm and house evolved as an
elemental combination of
wood, stone and earth.
Mildewed timber walls framed
rough planking floorboards,
encroached with stony soil.
Emotive pieces of furniture
were ranged in a ritual
formation.'

Greenwich Theatre, London,
1987
Director Patrick Mason
Lighting Mick Hughes
*Production photograph by Joe
Vanek*
Carmen du Sautoy (Abbie), Tom
Hickey (Ephraim)

44   The School for Scandal. Sheridan

DESIGNER CHRISTOPHER MORLEY: 'First images for a costume often spring from the personality of the performer. When they do, they tend to be right, and fit like a glove. I'm not sure how I'd dress another Mrs Candour, but Beryl Reid as that character was an image quite clear to me.'

Theatre Royal, Haymarket, 1983
Director John Barton
Lighting Brian Harris
Production photograph by Zoë Dominic

45   A Midsummer Night's Dream. Shakespeare

COSTUME DESIGNER PRISCILLA TRUETT: 'A concept of the fairies – this is Puck (David Whitaker) – as something ethereal or fantastic was rejected and they were seen, because of the Titania/Hippolyta Oberon/Theseus dual casting, as darker mirror images of the protagonists.'

Royal Shakespeare Company (tour and The Other Place), 1983/4
Director Sheila Hancock
Set designer Bob Crowley
Lighting Brian Harris

47

47

47 Hard Shoulder. Stephen Fagan

SET DESIGNER TANYA McCALLIN: 'This is the set in its Act 1 Scene 1 position: the roof of a derelict terrace house in north London. The architect, David, is inspecting the site. The set opened to reveal the first-floor interior, pre-set underneath.'

Hampstead Theatre, London, 1983
Director Nancy Meckler
Costume designer Sheelagh Killeen
Lighting Robert Ornbo
Production photograph by John Haynes
Peter Blythe (David), Susan Jameson (Johanna)

46 As You Like It.
Shakespeare

DESIGNER DI SEYMOUR:
'The exiled lords in the wintry forest. Nick recalled school camps – wet, cold, yet somehow happy. The lords share their meagre food with strangers. Theatre-in-the-round, so the audience is included in the warm circle around the fire. The seven ages of man is spoken in dancing firelight.'

Royal Exchange Theatre, Manchester, 1986
Director Nicholas Hytner
Lighting Paul Pyant
Production photograph by Kevin Cummins
Includes from left: Raad Rawi (Jacques), William Osborne (Amiens), Stuart Richman (Duke Senior)

48 'Tis Pity She's a Whore. John Ford

SET DESIGNER ROGER GLOSSOP: 'The setting was conceived for the Olivier's stage revolve, and enabled the 27 scenes of Ford's play to flow horizontally and vertically, clockwise and anti-clockwise. All areas could be used by the actors except for the topmost tower and staircase.'

National Theatre (Olivier), 1988
Director Alan Ayckbourn
Costume designer Sally Gardner
Lighting Mick Hughes
Set photograph by Dee Conway

49A 49B 49C 49D

49A–D **Hamlet**. Shakespeare

DESIGNER MARIA BJÖRNSON: 'A cool, analytical design was wanted, mixed with double exposure. Photographic clouds were used on glass, curtains, and the floor, as well as a sharp perspective. For the Gravedigger scene the whole floor split to reveal mud and puddles underneath.'

49A–D Ophelia's mad scene; the Court; the Queen's bedchamber; the Gravedigger scene

Royal Shakespeare Company, 1984
Director Ron Daniels
Lighting Chris Ellis
Set photographs by Joe Cocks Studio

50

50 **As You Like It**.
Shakespeare

DESIGNER BOB CROWLEY:
'Touchstone, Celia and
Rosalind are walking from the
harsh, oppressive world of the
Court to the abstract space,
fantasy and colour of the forest
– which I designed with no
trees. We were reacting
against any false rustic
references in the forest
scenes.'

Royal Shakespeare Company,
1985
Director Adrian Noble
Lighting Robert Bryan
*Production photograph by Donald
Cooper*
Nicky Henson (Touchstone),
Fiona Shaw (Celia), Juliet
Stevenson (Rosalind)

51 **King Lear**. Shakespeare

DESIGNER BOB CROWLEY:
'Lear and the Fool were seen
at times as literally a double-
act in theatrical terms.'

Royal Shakespeare Company,
1982
Director Adrian Noble
Lighting Brian Harris
*Production photograph by Donald
Cooper*
Antony Sher (the Fool), Michael
Gambon (Lear)

51

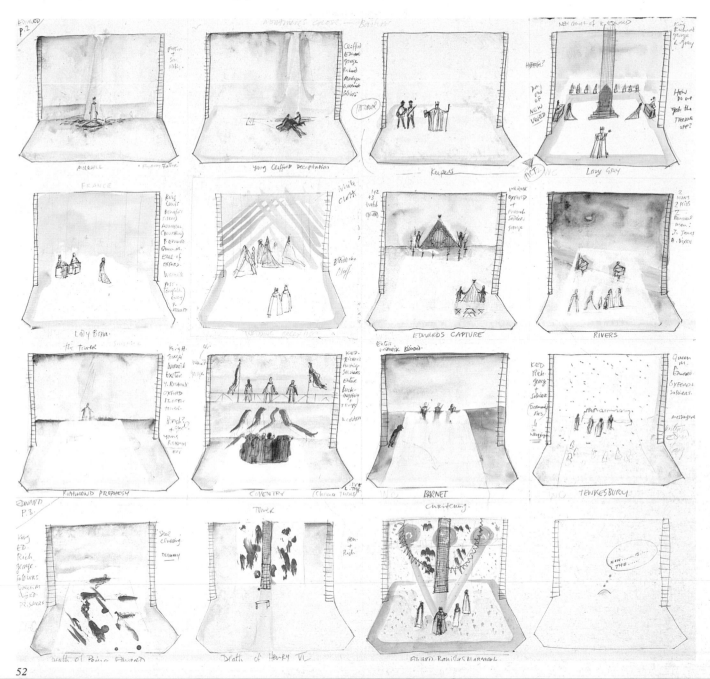

52 The Plantagenets:
Henry VI, The Rise of Edward IV and *Richard III, his Death.*
Shakespeare, adaptation of *Henry VI* (Parts 1–3) and *Richard III*

DESIGNER BOB CROWLEY:
'The trilogy had in all about a hundred scenes. This is my storyboard for those in *Edward IV*. I find actors and technicians respond to a storyboard with greater interest than they do to a model. Perhaps drawings – which I enjoy doing – capture the mood of a play better.'

Royal Shakespeare Company, 1988
Director Adrian Noble
Lighting Chris Parry

53 Henry V. Shakespeare

DESIGNER BOB CROWLEY:
'The élite of the French army before Agincourt, arrogant, proud, against a golden array of gleaming weapons.'

Royal Shakespeare Company, 1984
Director Adrian Noble
Lighting Robert Bryan
Production photograph by Donald Cooper
From left: Christopher Ravenscroft (Montjoy), Nicholas Woodeson (Dauphin), Ian Mackenzie (Orleans), Richard Easton (Constable of France)

54

54 **Schweyk in the Second World War**. Brecht, translation Susan Davies

COSTUME DESIGNER LINDY HEMMING: 'An "epic" production showing ordinary folk dwarfed by the monsters of the Third Reich. The nine-foot figures, evolved through a collaboration between Bill Dudley and myself, were actors on industrial stilts with moulded heads and uniforms built on strong but light foam sheeting to give the costumes body.'

National Theatre (Olivier), 1982
Director Richard Eyre
Set designer William Dudley
Lighting William Bundy
Production photograph by John Haynes
Jim Carter (Hitler), Bill Paterson (Schweyk)

55

56

55   A View from the Bridge. Arthur Miller

COSTUME DESIGNER LINDY HEMMING: 'The brief was accurately and unobtrusively to re-create the very worn and often washed work-wear of an Italian family in a Fifties American long-shore community – without the costumes looking like the modern Fifties style worn on the streets as fashion today.'

Costume drawing for Eddie Carbone (Michael Gambon)

National Theatre (Cottesloe), 1987
Director Alan Ayckbourn
Set designer Alan Tagg
Lighting Mick Hughes

56   Waiting for Godot. Beckett

COSTUME DESIGNER LINDY HEMMING: 'My inclination was to design costumes like those worn by the modern dispossessed who share the South Bank with the National Theatre. However, the brief was more traditional. The only things owned by Vladimir (Alec McCowen) and Estragon (John Alderton) are their clothes. These are constantly referred to, and tell us everything and nothing about the characters.'

Costume drawing for Vladimir

National Theatre (Lyttelton), 1987
Director Michael Rudman
Set designer William Dudley
Lighting Robert Bryan

57A

57B

57A & B   Measure for Measure. Shakespeare

DESIGNER MARK THOMPSON: 'We wanted a colossal image of state bureaucracy, and an old and new world coming together, creating an oppressive atmosphere. There were three main visual areas: the street (57A), the state and the prison. In the final act (57B) the sky was a token of troubled hope.'

Royal Shakespeare Company, 1987
Director Nicholas Hytner
Lighting Mark Henderson
Set photograph by Joe Cocks Studio (57A)
Production photograph by Clive Barda (57B)
Includes: Mark Dignam (Escalus), David Howey (Provost), Alex Jennings (Lucio), Roger Allam (Duke)

58A

58B

58A & B **Other Worlds**. Robert Holman

DESIGNER JOHN BYRNE: 'Apart from a kitchen set (flown in) the entire action was set outdoors –
on the seashore, and in the snow. I took my cue from the storm at sea at the beginning of the play in
which a sailing ship is wrecked. The 'sails', ripped and ragged, provided the simple box set I was
after; the snow was a white stagecloth; the lighting was brilliant.'

Royal Court Theatre, London, 1982
Director Richard Wilson
Lighting Matthew Richardson
Production photographs by John Haynes
Paul Copley (Joe)

59 **Candy Kisses**.
John Byrne

DESIGNER JOHN BYRNE: 'In
1963 I was in Perugia. It was
the coldest winter in European
living memory; the local
Italians sounded like
Dundonians; Italy had the
largest Communist party
outside the Soviet Union; and
many Americans were in
Perugia at the time their
president was murdered. All
this played a part in my work
in 1984 on *Candy Kisses*.'

Bush Theatre, London, 1984
Director Robin Lefevre
Lighting Gerry Jenkinson
*Production photograph by Nobby
Clark*
Mark Lambert (Alvarro)

59

60 **The Tempest**.
Shakespeare

DESIGNER RICHARD
HUDSON: 'The island was a
sandy textured pale yellow
slope, with dunes like rumpled
fabric against a deep blue
cyclorama. Prospero's cell and
the entrance from the sea were
open-ended cubes sinking into
the sand and thrusting
through the sky, tilted to give
the impression of having been
washed up by the sea.'

Old Vic, 1988
Director Jonathan Miller
Lighting Davy Cunningham
*Production photograph by Richard
Mildenhall*
Rudolph Walker (Caliban)

60

61 **Too Clever By Half**.
Ostrovsky, adaptation Rodney
Ackland

DESIGNER RICHARD
HUDSON: 'The set (the
picture shows it at the end of
the play) was steeply raked
and sharply tapered back with
leaning walls splattered. The
intended impression was of a
Moscow inhabited by
hypocrites and grotesques on
the verge of collapse.'

Old Vic, 1988
Director Richard Jones
Lighting Davy Cunningham
*Model photograph by Richard
Holttum*

61

62

62 **Man to Man**. Manfred Karge, translation Anthony Vivis

DESIGNER BUNNY CHRISTIE: 'The environment we wanted
to create was anonymous, sterile and ambiguous – a prison or
playroom within which Max Gericke could roam and where each
element of the set would read strongly. Seemingly random
costumes, props and furniture magically came to life during the
story.'

Traverse Theatre, Edinburgh, 1987
Director Stephen Unwin
Lighting Ben Ormerod
Production photograph by Sean Hudson
Tilda Swinton (Max Gericke)

63 **Way Upstream**.
Alan Ayckbourn

DESIGNER ALAN TAGG:
'The water-filled tank in
which this boat moved – on
rails beneath the surface – was
30 ft by 40 ft and deep as a
man. But the boat seen here,
the one used, is not the model
we wanted. That one, and the
factory adapting it, were burnt
in a fire just before rehearsals.
Also the tank leaked (until it
was put right) causing much
merriment in the media.'

National Theatre (Lyttelton),
1982
Director Alan Ayckbourn
Lighting William Bundy
*Production photograph by Nobby
Clark*
Jim Norton (Alistair), Julie
Legrand (Emma)

64 **Translations**.
Brian Friel

SET DESIGNER EILEEN DISS:
'Donegal in 1833 when the
Royal Engineers were doing a
map survey of Ireland,
changing Irish place names for
English ones. The characters,
Irish and English, gather in a
disused barn, now a "hedge
school", the only source of
education for the rural Irish.'

Hampstead Theatre, London,
1981
Director Donald McWhinnie
Costume designer Lindy
Hemming
Lighting Gerry Jenkinson and
Ronnie Cox
*Production photograph by John
Haynes*
From left: Sebastian Shaw
(Jimmy), Anna Keaveney
(Bridget), Bernadette Short
(Maire), Máire ní Ghráinne
(Sarah), Stephen Rea (Manus),
Ron Flanagan (Doalty)

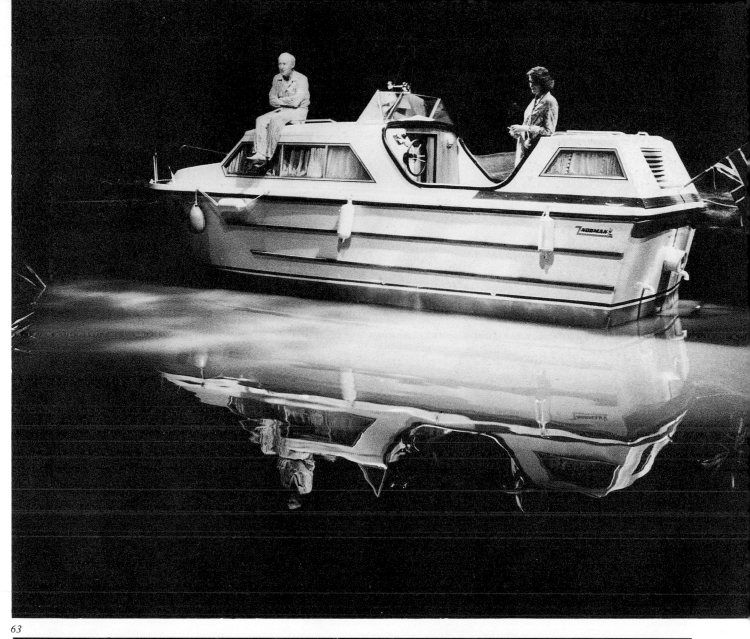

63

64

65A–D

65A–D **Betrayal**. Pinter

DESIGNER JOHN BURY: 'Small and intimate moments remembered – moving backwards through time. But never a clue as to a world outside those memories. The designer followed suit.'

National Theatre (Lyttelton), 1978
Director Peter Hall
Lighting John Bury
Set photographs by Group Three Photography

66 **Amadeus**. Peter Shaffer

DESIGNER JOHN BURY: 'A spoof about Salieri and Mozart, which had to be designed with great conviction and in strictest period, with not a hint that these things might never have happened.'

National Theatre (Olivier), 1979
Director Peter Hall
Lighting John Bury
Production photograph by Zoë Dominic
Simon Callow (Mozart), Paul Scofield (Salieri)

66

67 **Coriolanus**. Shakespeare

DESIGNER JOHN BURY: 'An attempt in that dangerous territory between historical accuracy and modern parallelism. Superb acting and direction saved the designer.'

National Theatre (Olivier), 1984
Director Peter Hall
Lighting John Bury
Production photograph by John Haynes
Downstage, centre:
Ian McKellen (Coriolanus)

67

68

69

68 The Art of Success. Nick Dear

DESIGNER ULTZ: 'A play about Hogarth and his world, about art and politics then and now. The actors were dressed in modern underwear glimpsed beneath 18th-century top clothes. It was performed in the round on a floating platform of paper-covered wood which became dirtied during the action. On the walls were Hogarth portraits in charcoal cross-hatching.'

Royal Shakespeare Company (The Other Place), 1986
Director Adrian Noble
Lighting Ian Loffhagen
Production photograph by Ivan Kyncl
From left: Niamh Cusack (Hogarth's wife), Michael Kitchen (Hogarth), Penny Downie (Jenny)

70

69 The Machine Wreckers. Ernst Toller, translation Peter Tegel

DESIGNER KENNY MILLER: 'The play dealt with the conflict between the manual industry of the period and the new era of machinery. I wanted to emphasize the humanity of the workers by placing them in an alien world of large spinning bobbins, and by hanging computer circuits in classical frames high above the stage.'

Glasgow Citizens Theatre, 1985
Director Giles Havergal
Lighting Gerry Jenkinson
Production photograph by John Vere Brown
Patrick Hannaway (Ned Lud)

70 Breaking the Code. Hugh Whitemore

DESIGNER LIZ DA COSTA: 'A composite set allowing episodic action within a machine-like environment evoking a wartime Nissen hut and an interrogation centre. Characters entering from the external world are glimpsed through the multi-openings along the back wall and sides. With Turing's final escape through suicide, the great doors open fully to reveal a sepia sky beyond.'

Theatre Royal, Haymarket, 1987
Director Clifford Williams
Lighting Mick Hughes
Production photograph by David Crosswaite
Derek Jacobi (Alan Turing), Joanna David (Pat Green)

Œdipus the King.   PRIEST

T.M.
Adelaide
Festival
1978

71A

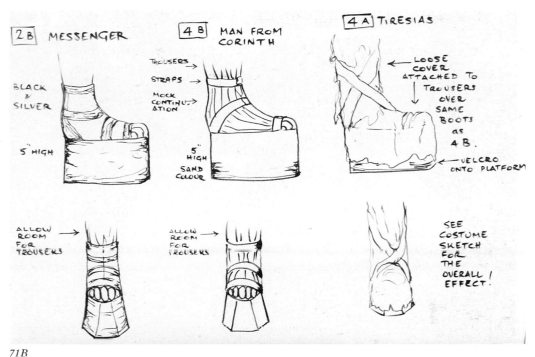

2B MESSENGER

BLACK & SILVER

5" HIGH

ALLOW ROOM FOR TROUSERS →

4B MAN FROM CORINTH

TROUSERS →
STRAPS →
MOCK CONTINU-ATION →

5" HIGH SAND COLOUR

ALLOW ROOM FOR TROUSERS →

4A TIRESIAS

← LOOSE COVER ATTACHED TO TROUSERS OVER SAME BOOTS as 4 B.

← VELCRO ONTO PLATFORM

SEE COSTUME SKETCH FOR THE OVERALL EFFECT.

71B

71A&B **Oedipus the King**.
Sophocles, translation John
Lewin

COSTUME DESIGNER TANYA
MOISEIWITSCH (masks as
well as costumes): 'The
enjoyment I get designing
comes from collaboration and
cooperation. In a way, this
project was homage paid by
Colin George [the play's
director] and me to our
memories of Tyrone Guthrie,
whose own work greatly
influenced mine.'

71A   Costume drawing for Priest

71B   Working drawings

South Australian Theatre
Company, Adelaide Festival of
Arts, 1978
Set designer Richard Roberts
Lighting Nigel Levings

72

72   **The Garden Girls**.
Jacqueline Holborough

DESIGNER GEOFF ROSE:
'This was a gift to do at The
Bush. It's just a room above a
pub but works unbelievably
well as a theatre. The main
part of the set was a formal
prison garden, so I laid a lawn
and flowerbeds. The really
hard work was done by the
stage management who had to
become devoted gardeners.'

Bush Theatre, London, 1986
Director Simon Stokes
Lighting Paul Denby
*Production photograph by Nobby
Clark*
Sophie Thompson (Dog),
Maureen O'Brien (Mary)

PLAYS

73 The Balcony. Genet, adaptation Barbara Wright
and Terry Hands

DESIGNER ABD' ELKADER FARRAH: 'A crimson house of
illusions whose customers have phantasms about power. A
revolution liquidating the real power. The bordello's clients
become the new power. Another revolution will liquidate them,
and so on . . . Reality? Illusion? It is a play full of clichés turned
into poetry, allegories, and rituals.'

Royal Shakespeare Company (Barbican), 1987
Director Terry Hands
Lighting Terry Hands with Clive Morris
Drawing photograph by Safi Farrah

73

74 Rutherford and Son.
Githa Sowerby

DESIGNER PENNY BROWN:
'The New End is a tiny
theatre, with the audience very
close. To achieve the realistic
clutter and claustrophobia of
this Victorian study without
being too overpowering, only
the important areas were in
full detail, the rest was faded
to black.'

New End Theatre, London, 1988
Director Wyn Jones
Lighting David I. Taylor and Sara
Pilling
Set photograph by Katie Vandyck

74

75 **The Roaring Girl**. Dekker

DESIGNER CHRIS DYER: 'This was an attempt to create an animated caricature of London, full of fun and visual texture; the end of one era, Elizabeth's, and the start of a very different one: of James I, puritanism, and the rise of a new mercantile class, greedy for wealth.'

Royal Shakespeare Company, 1983
Director Barry Kyle
Lighting Leo Leibovici
Set photograph, with stage crew, by Joe Cocks Studio

76 **King Lear**. Shakespeare

DESIGNER CHRIS DYER: 'The slab-stage, engraved as a map of Lear's kingdom, splits into three at the storm, and becomes an image of the play.'

Royal Shakespeare Company (The Other Place, an educational project), 1988
Director Cicely Berry
Lighting Robert Jones
Production photograph by Chris Dyer
Richard Haddon-Haines (Lear), Patrick Miller (The Fool)

75

76

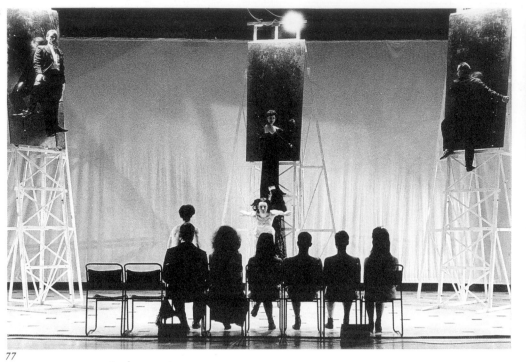

77

78

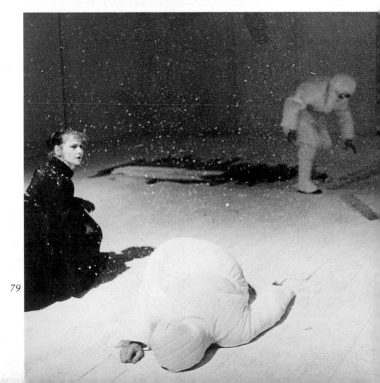

79

77 **The Sleep**. Devised by the company, words Clare Macdonald

DESIGNER SIMON VINCENZI: 'A space that used the idea of an operating theatre, where a woman's history is dissected and she is forced to watch images of her past.'

British tour, 1987
Director Pete Brooks
Production photograph by Alan Crumlish
Includes from left: Martin Nelson, Rachel Sherry, Mary Phillips, Reena Vetts, Michael Lee

78 **Savannah Bay**. Marguerite Duras, translation Barbara Bray

DESIGNER IONA McLEISH: 'The design came directly from the lyrical quality of the words, and the gaps between them. The very small stage surface was a pale oval space, encircled by mirror piled with smooth grey pebbles. The creamy curtains were on a circular steel track.'

Foco Novo, 1988
Director Susan Todd
Lighting Geraint Pughe
Production photograph by Iona McLeish
Alexandra Mathie (Young Woman), Faith Brook (Madeleine, holding curtain)

79 **Frankenstein**. Mary Shelley, adaptation Jonathan Pope

DESIGNER KATHY STRACHAN: 'The bare stage became the hold of a ship, a theatrical laboratory, and a snow-swept tundra. Floorboards were ripped up revealing expanses of water; panels were torn from riveted stanchions letting in floods of white light.'

Glasgow Citizens Theatre, 1988
Director Jonathan Pope
Lighting Gerry Jenkinson
Production photograph by John Vere Brown
Beatrice Comins (Mary Shelley)

80A & B **The Life of Galileo**. Brecht, translation Howard Brenton

DESIGNER JOCELYN HERBERT: 'The scaffolding was metal, the lighting grid was suspended above it, and the stage was a circle of wood planks. Light projections were used, and scenic elements were flown in or trucked on. The drawings (*80A*) are a selection from my storyboard. The set photograph (*80B*) shows the stage at the start and end of the play; the astrolabe, reflected each side, was a symbol of Galileo's work on astronomy.'

80A The basic set; Rome; the Ball; Galileo's house

National Theatre (Olivier), 1980
Director John Dexter
Lighting Andy Phillips
Set photograph by Group Three Photography (80B)

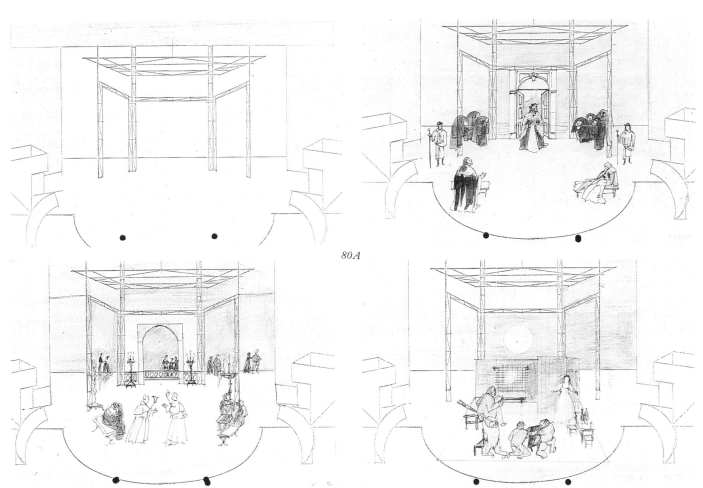

80A

80B

81 **The Rivals**. Sheridan

SET DESIGNER JOHN GUNTER: 'The joy of designing this play was to put the whole of Bath on the Olivier stage, with all the characters having their own houses.'

National Theatre (Olivier), 1983
Director Peter Wood
Costume designer Bruce Snyder
Lighting Robert Bryan
Set photograph by Zoë Dominic

82 **Maydays**. David Edgar

SET DESIGNER JOHN GUNTER: 'The problem with this design was having to go rapidly from the Hungarian uprising, to Frankfurt airport, to an English university, to a squat, to a train carrying arms in the United States, to Greenham Common (picture), and so on; plus passing through three decades.'

Royal Shakespeare Company, 1983
Director Ron Daniels
Costume designer Di Seymour
Lighting Chris Ellis
Production photograph by Donald Cooper
Antony Sher (Martin Glass)

82

83 **Lorenzaccio**. Alfred de Musset, translation and adaptation John Fowles

SET DESIGNER JOHN GUNTER: 'The play concerns a conspiratorial time in Florence, and the intention was to show it in turmoil and transition, a city of open street fighting and vandalism.'

National Theatre (Olivier), 1983
Director Michael Bogdanov
Costume designer Stephanie Howard
Lighting Chris Ellis
Production photograph by Laurence Burns
Centre: Stephen Hattersley (Pietro Strozzi)
Extreme right: Michael Bryant (Filippo Strozzi)

84 **The Government Inspector**. Gogol, version Adrian Mitchell

SET DESIGNER JOHN GUNTER: 'The action takes place in a backward little community which was but the merest cog in the vast Russian bureaucratic machine. So the set became no bigger, relatively, than the inkwell on a gigantic pile of official papers.'

National Theatre (Olivier), 1985
Director Richard Eyre
Costume designer Deirdre Clancy
Lighting David Hersey
Photograph photograph by John Haynes
From left: Jim Broadbent (Governor), Ivor Roberts (Judge), Peter Blythe (Charity Commissioner), Richard Hope (Postmaster), Fred Pearson (Schools' Superintendent)

83

84

85 **Saint Joan**. Shaw

SET DESIGNER JOHN
GUNTER

Working drawing for the siege
tower

National Theatre (Olivier), 1984
Director Ronald Eyre
Costume designers Sally Gardner
and John Gunter
Lighting Chris Ellis

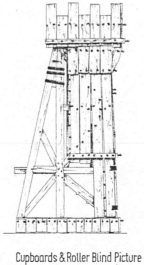
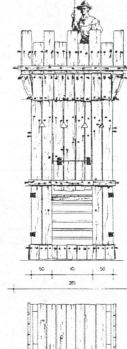
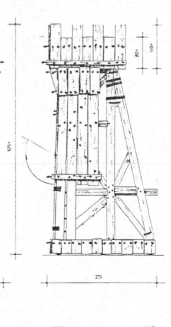

Cupboards & Roller Blind Picture

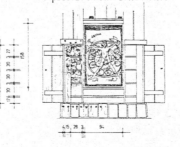
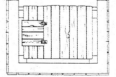

85

86

87

86 **Electra**. Sophocles, translation Kenneth McLeish

DESIGNER HILDEGARD BECHTLER: 'Seats were taken out to provide a courtyard big enough in the RSC's tiny Pit theatre for a Chorus of five and Electra to be on stage throughout. Dividing the courtyard was a gulley filled with water which eventually received Orestes's ashes and turned red with the blood of Clytemnestra. The set became marked and stained as the play moved on.'

Royal Shakespeare Company (The Pit), 1989
Director Deborah Warner
Lighting Geraint Pughe
Production photograph by Ivan Kyncl
Foreground from left: Fiona Shaw (Electra), Piers Ibbotson (Orestes). Behind them: Darlene Johnson (Chorus), Kate Littlewood (Chorus), Derek Hutchinson (Pylades)

87 **The Tourist Guide**. Botho Strauss, adaptation Anthony Vivis and Tinch Minter

DESIGNER HILDEGARD BECHTLER: 'Mythical Greece was expressed by a monolithic arch. Primary colours were brought in to startle and evoke images of violence in the mind.'

Almeida Theatre, London, 1987
Director Pierre Audi
Lighting Jean Kalman
Production photograph by Ivan Kyncl
Tilda Swinton (Kristine), Paul Freeman (Martin)

88A & B As You Desire Me.
Pirandello, translation Marius
Ploritis

DESIGNER NICHOLAS
GEORGIADIS: 'It seemed to
me that in the mind of the
central character, the
Unknown Woman, the
geography of the settings for
the two acts should be
identical, but that the first
should look like a negative of
the second.'

88A Costume design for the
Unknown Woman

88B Model for Act 2

Lambetti Theatre, Athens, 1986
Director Jane Howell
Lighting Jane Howell and
Nicholas Georgiadis
*Model photograph by Iris
Argyropoulos (88B)*

88A

88B

89A

89B

89A & B **The Wandering Jew**. Michelene Wandor and Mike Alfreds, adaptation of novel by Eugene Sue

DESIGNER PAUL DART: 'The main brief was for the set to have a basic permanent construction yet to be completely flexible: to empty, or to fill with drapes; and with the actors partly creating the design while presenting the story.'

89A Drawing of permanent construction

National Theatre (Olivier), 1987
Director Mike Alfreds
Lighting Paul Dart
Production photograph by John Haynes (89B)
From left: Pip Donaghy, Kate Godfrey, Paola Dionisotti, Brian Badcoe, Sian Thomas, Lucien Taylor, Susanna Bishop, Philip Voss, Mark Rylance

90 **The Last Supper**. Howard Barker

DESIGNER DERMOT HAYES: 'The setting is a ruined cathedral in desolate country towards the end of a long war. The door is surrounded by a cracked, worn landscape painted on to old canvas strung up like a tarpaulin. It represents something precious and once beautiful which has become worthless.'

Royal Court Theatre, London, 1988
Director Kenny Ireland
Lighting Andy Phillips
Production photograph by John Haynes
From left: Hugh Fraser (Arnold), Jane Bertish (Marya), Philip Sayer (Lvov)

91 **Steaming**. Nell Dunn

DESIGNER JENNY TIRAMANI: 'The play took place in different parts of a public bath-house. To help make each individual area more convincing, we used real furnishings and fittings from an actual bath-house that was being demolished at the time.'

Theatre Royal, Stratford East, London, 1981
Director Roger Smith
Lighting Mick Hughes
Set photograph by John Gorringe
A member of staff prepares the set

92 **Shadow of a Gunman**. O'Casey

DESIGNER MARTYN BAINBRIDGE: 'The play is set in Dublin in 1920, before partition, and the setting was basically naturalistic, with the continuing tragedy of Ireland evoked by modern photographic images on a map of the country.'

Theatre Royal, Plymouth, 1986
Director Roger Redfarn
Lighting David H. Cohen
Set photograph by Martyn Bainbridge

90

91

92

93A & B

94A & B

93A & B **Rough Crossing**. Stoppard, adaption of *Play at the Castle* by Molnar

DESIGNER CARL TOMS: 'The play is set in the 1930s on a luxury liner, and the designs showed, I hope, an ironical witty view of the nautical style then, not merely a pastiche. Both acts called for fast, open, choreographed scene changes.'

National Theatre (Lyttelton), 1984
Director Peter Wood
Lighting David Hersey
Set photographs by Group Three Photography

94A & B **On the Razzle**. Stoppard, adaptation of *Einen dux will er sich machen* by Nestroy

DESIGNER CARL TOMS: 'A complicated fast-moving farce involving five sets which had to change in view: two large carrying platforms tracked diagonally up and down stage, one masking the other when it was in place. Flying pieces completed the set.'

National Theatre (Lyttelton), 1981
Director Peter Wood
Lighting Robert Bryan
Set photographs by Group Three Photography

95 The Pied Piper. Adrian Mitchell, from Browning's poem

COSTUME DESIGNER SALLY GARDNER: 'This costume had to incorporate a feeling of patchwork past and present. Adrian Mitchell's song that described how the Pied Piper got his patches was my key. I was after a magical, mysterious Pied Piper of the Eighties.'

National Theatre (Olivier), 1986
Devised and directed by Alan Cohen
Set designer Roger Glossop
Lighting Paul McLeish

96 The Women. Clare Boothe Luce

SET DESIGNER VOYTEK: 'I set the play as an art-deco glitzy cage, turning into an even glitzier jungle, and housing eighteen women, New York cats, fighting each other to the death of their marriages. The picture shows the most predatory of all in her cage/bathroom.'

Yvonne Arnaud Theatre, Guildford, 1986
Director Keith Hack
Costume designer John Bright
Lighting Durham Marenghi
Production photograph by Joe Roman
Georgina Hale (Crystal)

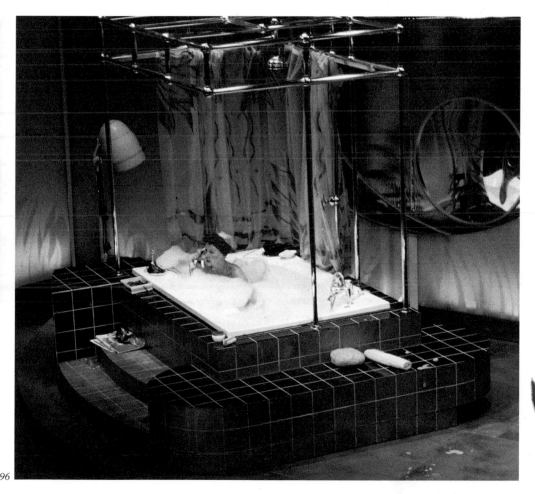

96

95

97A 97B 99

97A & B   The Taming of the Shrew. Shakespeare

COSTUME DESIGNER MARTIN CHITTY: 'There was a lot of serious talk about whether Petruchio's wedding get-up – seen here are design (*97A*) and stage realization (*97B*) – was funny enough. But in the event it worked, getting a roar of laughter at the first night.'

Royal Shakespeare Company, 1987
Director Jonathan Miller
Set designer Stefanos Lazaridis
Lighting Davy Cunningham
Production photograph by Joe Cocks Studio
Brian Cox (Petruchio)

98   Mountain Language. Pinter

DESIGNER MICHAEL TAYLOR: 'The play is set in a military prison for "enemies of the state", in England as it might be. It moves through four vivid scenes (gate, cell, corridor, back to cell) in 22 minutes. The setting was simple, English, and prison-like without the associations of actual prison architecture.'

National Theatre (Lyttelton), 1988
Director Harold Pinter
Lighting Laurence Clayton
Production photograph by Ivan Kyncl
Includes from centre (to right): Miranda Richardson (Young Woman), Eileen Atkins (Elderly Woman), Michael Gambon (Sergeant), Julian Wadham (Officer)

99   A Man For All Seasons. Robert Bolt

DESIGNER JULIA TREVELYAN OMAN: 'A permanent set as the 1987 solution for a play written in 1960, to be performed on the thrust stage of a theatre built in 1962. A reconception of Renaissance elements, to give an architectural screen suitable for many locations with minimum use of drapes and properties.'

Chichester Festival Theatre, 1987
Director Frank Hauser
Lighting Leonard Tucker
Set photograph by Reg Wilson

98

100   **The Taming of the Shrew**. Shakespeare

SET DESIGNER STEFANOS LAZARIDIS: 'The marquetry effect of the wooden set created different aspects of perspective. The side walls concealed wood panels which tracked on and off the stage, expanding and contracting the depth of the space. A cobalt blue sky could be seen through various apertures.'

Royal Shakespeare Company, 1987
Director Jonathan Miller
Costume designer Martin Chitty
Lighting Davy Cunningham
Model photograph by Clive Barda

101 Treasure Island.
Stevenson, adaptation James
Maxwell

COSTUME DESIGNER DAVID
SHORT: 'Abraham Gray,
ship's carpenter, a character
little described and with few
lines: an opportunity, that was
a joy, to invent an identity for
him.'

Royal Exchange Theatre,
Manchester, 1981
Director James Maxwell
Set designer Laurie Dennett
Lighting Glyn Peregrine

Abraham Grey
'Treasure Island'

101

102 Hope against Hope.
Adaptation Casper Wrede
from writings of Osip
Mandelstam

COSTUME DESIGNER DAVID
SHORT: 'These people
symbolize the many constantly
being forced into exile and
shunted from one small God-
forsaken town to another
during the years of Stalin.
Mandelstam, a great Russian
poet, and his wife lived
through that time.'

Royal Exchange Theatre,
Manchester, 1983
Director Casper Wrede
Set designer Stephen McCabe
Lighting Michael Williams

Exiles on a Pier
'Hope Against Hope'

102

103

103 American Buffalo.
David Mamet

DESIGNER GRANT HICKS:
'The set represented a
Chicago basement junk and
second-hand shop. Thousands
of props dressed the set,
genuine Americana for the
most part, which had to be
"trashed-up".'

National Theatre (Cottesloe),
1978
Director Bill Bryden
Lighting Andy Phillips
*Production photograph by Nobby
Clark*
Dave King (Don), Jack Shepherd
(Teach)

104

104 The Slab Boys.
John Byrne

DESIGNER GRANT HICKS:
'This is the slab room, where
the colours for a carpet factory
were ground and prepared. It
was the small back room of a
much larger factory, and I
wanted to convey this, as well
as an authentic Fifties
environment. The audience
sat on three sides. The
production was a successful
collaboration between writer,
director and designer.'

Traverse Theatre, Edinburgh,
1978
Director David Hayman
Lighting Alastair McArthur
*Production photograph by Grant
Hicks*
From left: Pat Doyle (Hector), Jim
Byars (Spanky), Billy McColl
(Phil), Freddie Boardley (Alan)

105

105 **Blood Wedding**. Lorca, translation Gwynne Edwards

DESIGNER NETTIE EDWARDS: 'My original costume designs were simple and primitive (as here) but in response to rehearsals they became more ornate and ceremonial.'

Costume design for The Mother

Contact Theatre, Manchester, 1988
Director Anthony Clark
Lighting Stephen Henbest

106

108A

106 **Heart-throb**. Caroline Hutchison, Anna Mottram, Jeremy Seabrook

DESIGNER JULIAN McGOWAN: 'The play is set in a New Town flat – so to achieve an element of realism I used plasterboard and chipboard in the design. Then a heavy session of breaking down gave the effect of decay due to damp and neglect.'

Bush Theatre, London, 1988
Director Richard Wilson
Lighting Kevin Sleep
Production photograph by Nobby Clark
Anna Mottram (Francine)

107 **Sore Points**. Bryony Lavery

DESIGNER MARSHA RODDY: 'Many Parts is a frenzied, bright, magical character who is ever-changing. I represented this through colour, texture and movement, using a mixture of Oriental painting and child-like image.'

Unicorn Children's Theatre, 1986
Director Simon Van der Borgh

107

108A & B **Faust** (Parts 1 & 2). Goethe, English version Robert David MacDonald

DESIGNER DAVID ROGER: 'In a production dominated by the four alchemical elements, one of them – water – characterized the climax of Walpurgisnight (*108A*), with the eruption of five fountains, a rain curtain, and the slow flooding of three forestage tanks.'

'Euphorion, son of Faust and Helen, attempts to reach the sun (*108B*). The arched ladder was constant throughout the two evenings of thirty-four scenes, an image of man's continual journeying between earthbound and heavenbound desires.'

Lyric Theatre, Hammersmith, 1988
Director David Freeman
Lighting Peter Mumford
Production photographs by Donald Cooper
108A Robyn Moore (Galatea), Linda Kerr Scott (Homunculus, in bubble)
108B Simon Callow (Faust, on ladder), Graham Walters (Euphorion), Caroline Bliss (Helen of Troy)

108B

110 Macbeth. Shakespeare

COSTUME DESIGNER POPPY MITCHELL: 'The brief for the costume designs was to reflect the world of the Eighties. The witches' clothes were put together out of an assortment of old garments and bits and pieces to resemble the modern, rather sinister "bag ladies" who pick around in a twilight world of other people's leftovers.'

Royal Shakespeare Company, 1982
Director Howard Davies
Set designer Chris Dyer
Lighting Howard Eaton
Production photograph by Donald Cooper
From left: Katy Behean, Christine Kavanagh, Josette Simon

109

109 **Amabel**. Terry Johnson

DESIGNER POPPY MITCHELL: 'The Bush Theatre is basically just a large room with seating. The brief was to recreate in this tiny space the artists' world of the Paris of the 1890s, with scenes in studios, brothels, and outside locations. The walls of the acting area were covered in canvas painted to look like a Degas.'

Bush Theatre, London, 1979
Director Simon Stokes
Lighting Chris O'May
Production photograph by Nobby Clark
From left: Di Trevis (Eve), Julia Blalock (Louise), Angela Chadfield (Suzanne)

110

111

111 **The Tempest**. Shakespeare

DESIGNER DAVID FIELDING: 'The Masque. Prospero conjures his vision of a harmonious universe for Miranda and Ferdinand. From his cell, at the centre of an oval planked disc, emerge Iris, Juno and Ceres with their Shadows. In the background the clouds rise to reveal reapers dancing in a pastoral landscape.'

Royal Shakespeare Company, 1988
Director Nicholas Hytner
Lighting Mark Henderson
Production photograph by Clive Barda
From left: James Purefoy (Ferdinand), Melanie Thaw (Miranda), John Wood (Prospero, lying down), Duncan Bell (Ariel.)

112

112 **Princess Ivona**.
Gombrovicz, translation
Krystyna Griffith-Jones and
Catherine Robins

DESIGNER LEZ
BROTHERSTON:
'Gombrovicz was deeply
interested in the facets there
are to a person: to a friend we
are one personality, to an
employer someone different.
Our production was an
attempt to reveal the public
and private fixations and
doubts in a court troubled
with secrets and vices. Behind
the façade of public pomp lie
loneliness and guilt.'

Actors Touring Company, 1988
Director Mark Brickman
Lighting Guy Retallack
*Production photograph by David
Corio*
From left: Stephen Caro
(Chamberlain), Phoebe Burridge
(Isabelle), Ian Jeffs (Cyprian),
Terence Beesley (King), Sharon
Bower (Queen), Kevin
O'Donohoe (Philip), Emma
Dewhurst (Ivona), Andrew Celli
(Simon).

113

113 **King Lear**. Shakespeare

SET DESIGNER HAYDEN
GRIFFIN: 'One of my
storyboard drawings of the
play, scene by scene, based on
the decision to use three
enormous cloths, which
increased the vertical space of
the Olivier stage.'

National Theatre (Olivier), 1986
Director David Hare
Costume designer Christine
Stromberg
Lighting Rory Dempster

114 **Glengarry Glen Ross**.
David Mamet

DESIGNER HAYDEN
GRIFFIN: 'The second act,
the office after the break-in,
with the broken window
boarded up. The actors are lit
entirely by overhead office
lights; no normal theatre
lighting, such as spots etc, was
used.'

National Theatre (Cottesloe),
1983
Director Bill Bryden
Lighting Andy Phillips
*Production photograph by Nobby
Clark*
From left. Derek Newark (Shelly),
Jack Shepherd (Richard), Tony
Haygarth (James), James Grant
(George), John Tams (Baylen),
Karl Johnson (John)

114

115 **Pravda**. Howard
Brenton and David Hare

SET DESIGNER HAYDEN
GRIFFIN: 'David Hare and I
wanted to create the long
horizontal scale of a
newsroom, but also to
condense the main action of
the scene. The two diagonals
thrust the centre acting area
towards the audience.'

National Theatre (Olivier), 1985
Director David Hare
Costume designer Lindy
Hemming
Lighting Rory Dempster
*Set photograph by Group Three
Photography*

115

OPERA

JOHN HIGGINS

Not many people recognized it, but the end of the Seventies saw the face of opera on stage in Britain beginning to change. Until then much of the designing for the lyric theatre, especially in London, was basically decorative. The chocolate-box analogy was one of the critical clichés of the time. A general administrator, looking back on those days, recently remarked: 'It wasn't opera; it was a concert in frocks.'

That rather overstates the case, but there was certainly an audience which went to Covent Garden and the Coliseum expecting to see the production values of Shaftesbury Avenue or, say, the Haymarket writ large. The spirit of Oliver Messel – an admirable one in the right context – was still in the air with the work of men like Peter Rice, David Walker and Tony Walton among others. At the Royal Opera House Götz Friedrich was introducing the new German school of hard black and white sets, not always successfully. There will be few happy memories of a trouble-struck *Idomeneo* in 1978 or indeed of the revival of the Friedrich interpretation of *Freischütz*, where Weber's jolly Ländlers and hunting choruses rang out against a leafless forest of apparently napalmed trees. There were also that September three complete cycles of the Friedrich/Svoboda *Ring*; and with it the usual arguments following any *Ring* production, this time about the way it compared with one Ralph Koltai had designed for Glen Byam Shaw and John Blatchley at the Coliseum.

But for Italian opera, Covent Garden still lived at least half in the world of two masters who had changed our visual perceptions of the art over the previous twenty years: Franco Zeffirelli and his mentor, Luchino Visconti. Zeffirelli's stagings of both *Rigoletto* and *Falstaff* were also to be seen in 1978; Visconti was represented by *Trovatore*, with *Don Carlos* waiting in the wings.

116

116 **Hansel and Gretel**. Humperdinck

DESIGNER STEFANOS LAZARIDIS

The Angels' sequence

English National Opera, 1987
Director David Pountney
Lighting Chris Ellis
Production photograph by Clive Barda
Norman Bailey (the Father, centre), Felicity Palmer (the Mother)

The year had begun with a revival of Puccini's *La Fanciulla del West*, first seen the previous May. This will probably be considered the last of Covent Garden's home-grown spectaculars. Piero Faggioni's production was very much of the Zeffirelli school: detailed and realistic from the timbered bar run by Minnie, the girl of the Golden West, through to the mining canyon of the last act, where a massive water wheel began to revolve only during the closing moments of the opera. A fellow Italian, Ezio Frigerio, provided the costumes, but the sets were by a Briton, Ken Adam, who came in from the cinema where he had had a long acquaintance with the James Bond films. Other heavyweight productions were to follow, *L'Africaine* and *Lucrezia Borgia* among them. But nothing in the next decade was to match the grandeur of *Fanciulla*.

The following year at the Coliseum there was another watershed in the way Italian opera was to be approached: the *Aida* directed by John Copley and designed by Stefanos Lazaridis. Copley was the

117   **The Turn of the Screw**. Britten

DESIGNERS PATRICK ROBERTSON and ROSEMARY VERCOE

English National Opera 1979
Director Jonathan Miller
Lighting David Hersey
Production photograph by Patrick Robertson
From left: Ava June (Mrs Grose), Iris Saunders (Flora), Eilene Hannan (the Governess)

117

supreme technician and not for nothing had he learnt at the feet of Zeffirelli and others at Covent Garden. He knew how to present his singers in the very best (and most comfortable) light on stage. He went through the score meticulously with his designers, on whom he had a considerable influence. He was like a teacher guiding his students with a batch of old recordings, analysing how each effect was achieved. But this *Aida*, for all its opulence, was not a success. It was criticized, justly, for being grand opera gone wild, with gold paint everywhere and cumbersome sets which restricted the singing area – to say nothing of the dancing area. Lazaridis remembers that it was for him almost the end of the decorative phase in opera. When he designed the touring company version a year later, directed by Nicholas Hytner, he threw out virtually all of his earlier visual concepts. But that did not work either. When *Aida* returned at the beginning of the 1980–1 season as an amalgam of the two versions, and with marked adjustments to the ballet, it remained cumbersome. An operatic white elephant despite all the gold.

Economy, fuelled by the continuing financial crises of practically every opera house in the country, had already by the late 1970s become the new watchword. Jonathan Miller, working with his usual design team of Patrick Robertson and Rosemary Vercoe, had set his face against all ostentation from his early days at Kent Opera. There was nothing flashy about his *Marriage of Figaro* for the Coliseum (1978); and the far more evocative *Turn of the Screw* at the same house (1979) produced its effects with a bare minimum of scenery and the plentiful use of screens and projections.

However, probably the most influential of the new 'economic' productions was Covent Garden's *Peter Grimes*, directed by Elijah Moshinsky, designed by Timothy O'Brien and Tazeena Firth. It was there on view at the Royal Opera House in 1979, covered with accolades for its imaginativeness and its cheapness. *Grimes* was the supreme example of invention mothered by necessity. Covent Garden had been invited to make their first visit to La Scala and were keen to put *Grimes* in the repertoire. The only problem was that the existing production was falling to bits and would almost certainly not have managed the journey. The production–design team was allowed only half the normal production budget, as well as having to give a formal guarantee that it would not be exceeded. O'Brien and Firth used an open set, which was in effect a slice of the Aldeburgh foreshore. It was a mixture of real and manufactured materials: sand, duckboard and pebbles. Costumes were plundered from other productions and *Grimes* was brought in on budget: a lasting visual and economic success.

But even before the first night O'Brien and Firth were well aware of the dangers of this approach. Asked before the opening if this would lead to more invitations to refurbish ailing parts of the repertoire O'Brien replied succinctly that they had no intention of getting a reputation of being a cut-price operation. And he stuck to his word. The Covent Garden *Otello* was probably his single most expensive design. However, other Intendants were quick to recognize the achievement of *Grimes*; it was after all no more than what some of the grandest German houses and directors had already been doing before the *Wirtschaftswunder* released sacks of civic gold. Wieland Wagner had not actually overburdened Bayreuth with scenery. Architectural values were more important than decorative ones. In East Berlin too, especially at the Komische Oper, mighty effects had been produced often with the minimum of material. *Grimes* cleansed a few minds, but it also encouraged a few others to preach cheapness as an asset.

Probably *Grimes*'s most important progeny was the Norwest-Holst series at the Coliseum in the early Eighties. The sponsors put up the money for 'disposable' stagings of operas which deserved an airing but which could not be expected to command a regular place in the repertoire. The production team was told to use its imagination to bring in a very low-cost piece of theatre – £25,000 was the norm – and it was given the freedom to scavenge anything from the storeroom. The designers were to be almost Autolycuses, snapping up unconsidered trifles. But there was one crucial difference: *Grimes* was built to last and it did, while the Norwest productions were to vanish for ever after their allotted run of performances.

The first was Wagner's *Rienzi*, which opened in September 1983. It brought together for the first time in a major London house the team of director Nicholas Hytner and designer David Fielding. Not everyone liked the results, especially Hytner's fascist updating of the piece. But the experiment was generally reckoned 'a good thing'. The same was certainly not said about the next production, Tchaikovsky's *Mazeppa*, a year later. Fielding was again the designer, but this time David Alden the director. It quickly became known as the 'Chain Saw Massacre *Mazeppa*' both because of the violence introduced on stage and the lurid set, which might have begun in a rehearsal room but moved on fast from there. On the first night there was a considerable amount of booing, an unusual sound in a house known for the loyalty and warmth of its audience. But one which was to become more frequent. The final work of the series, Rossini's *Moses*, fared little better. It was a mess, beginning with the designs by the young Romanian, Marie-Jeanne Lecca, who had come to live in Britain and done a good job on Catalani's *La Wally* for the Wexford Festival.

At this point the experiment was stopped and the Coliseum started to analyse its costs and benefits. Certainly it had established Fielding as a powerful and unpredictable force in London. Before then much of his work had been done for Scottish Opera and the Welsh National Opera (WNO). There was no Fielding trademark: he was capable of turning *Rigoletto* for Scottish Opera into a punkish denunciation of moral squalor as well as abetting the excesses of *Mazeppa* at the Coliseum, but he could also devise a set as light and airy as that for Opera North's *Beatrice and Benedict*, or as dark and louring as the one for the Wexford Festival's justly praised staging of Marschner's *Hans Heiling*. No one was too surprised when in 1985 David Fielding provided what was probably the decade's single most elegant set seen at the Coliseum, that for Handel's *Xerxes*, a dazzle of white and green topiary with costumes to match. Nicholas Hytner was again the director and it became clear that Fielding worked best under his restraining hand.

The debit side of the Norwest-Holst experiment was the encouragement it gave designers to be adven-

118

turous at all costs. That cost was frequently at the expense of the intentions of the composer and librettists. A quite different and rather more solid sort of innovation had been emerging for some time at both the WNO and Scottish Opera, often in collaboration. Brian McMaster had arrived at the WNO as General Administrator in the summer of 1976, after a period as controller of planning at the ENO. McMaster, most retiring of Intendants, was not a man for the public statement; but it soon became clear that he was going to drag Wales into the final quarter of the twentieth century in production terms. Moreover he was going to give it a taste of Europe. Soon he was prowling around the European houses on both sides of the Iron Curtain, especially those with a reputation for the avant-garde: he was more likely to be seen at Darmstadt than at La Scala, or at East Berlin's Komische Oper rather than at the Vienna State. The result was that directors like Harry Kupfer and Joachim Herz made their British débuts in Cardiff.

McMaster also noted that the director–designer

118   **The Cunning Little Vixen**. Janáček

DESIGNER MARIA BJÖRNSON

Scottish Opera, 1980
Director David Pountney
Lighting Nick Chelton

combination of David Pountney and Maria Björnson was fast establishing a reputation with Scottish Opera in the East European repertoire. Pountney had first come to the attention at Wexford with an intense and imaginative *Katya Kabanova*. The second half of the Seventies saw his *Golden Cockerel* and *Bartered Bride*. Maria Björnson and Sue Blane shared costumes and sets in both cases, which brought a touch of the exotic, not through heavyweight sets but via bold, almost Russian colour in the Wakhevitch style. At the same time Pountney and Björnson were considering a major Janáček cycle.

Wales started it off with a highly successful *Jenufa* in 1975, and in September 1978 (the first season to reflect the McMaster taste properly) followed it with Janáček's most exotic and probably most difficult opera, *The Makropulos Case*. Cardiff had never seen a set quite like that provided by Björnson – the piled legal tomes of the office, where the legal case of the title is conducted, pierced by jagged Expressionist lighting. This was a touch of the European theatre,

94

even if some of it was deliberately dated to the time of Karel Capek, who provided Janáček's libretto. *The Cunning Little Vixen*, *Katya Kabanova* and *From the House of the Dead*, which followed for Scottish Opera or WNO, or for both, fully cemented the Pountney–Björnson partnership. The Janáček cycle almost certainly moulded much of Pountney's thinking on staging and design for his move south; he eventually left Scottish Opera to come to the ENO as director of productions on the arrival as music director of Mark Elder – his Cambridge friend and contemporary.

Although the biggest artistic splashes tended to be made at the WNO by the foreign teams, McMaster's eyes were not always turned to Europe or to partnerships with Scottish Opera. In January 1982 Mold (scarcely a very major date even in the WNO calendar) saw a production of Handel's *Tamerlano* – not a title at the forefront of most opera-goers' minds. The critics complained about struggling through the snow, but they did see the first opera to be both designed and directed by Philip Prowse. He used his favourite shades of grey for a stunning set of a palace dominated by two equestrian statues and surrounded by the ruins of war. The cool, almost ironic Prowse approach did not please all Handelians, but the sense of style could not be ignored.

Nor now can be Prowse's influence on opera design. Sue Blane learned much from him at the Citizens Theatre in Glasgow, Prowse's home base. So did Maria Björnson, one of the most prolific of opera designers before she was swept into productions in the upper financial stratosphere – for Andrew Lloyd Webber's Really Useful Company. Prowse himself did not stop with *Tamerlano*. In 1986 he again played the dual role of director–designer, with a 'Victorian' *Aida* for Opera North; it was sumptuous – no shades of grey this time. There were one or two directorial miscalculations, some of which were cleaned up on revival, but Prowse leapt over that stumbling block, which had produced so many casualties before, that of putting on a very grand opera in a small theatre. There was too, among other Prowse productions, a *Pearl Fishers* for the ENO, highly decorative but somewhat static. That though, some would say, is the

fault of Bizet and his librettists.

Prowse, despite his fairly small operatic output, remains one of the few designers in lyric theatre also prepared to direct. On the Continent the combination is quite common. The supreme example is the late Jean-Pierre Ponnelle, who quickly decided that he could do just as well as the directors with whom he had been working as designer. He succeeded. Ponnelle's productions – and he was rarely seen at his best in Britain – had a unity, wit and musicality that were unmistakable. Sandro Sequi, Ezio Frigerio, Achim Freyer and Pier Luigi Pizzi are obvious examples of others wearing a double hat. Why then do not more in this country take the same trail?

'Absolute terror' was the reply of one designer, adding that there was some mystique about the role of the opera director, including a need to understand the mysterious ways and moods of opera singers. Be that as it may, I would guess that in the future more designers will chance their hand at the mystic art. Indeed, some have been doing so already, including Stefanos Lazaridis, when Opera North revived Stravinsky's *Oedipus Rex*. David Fielding tried his hand at Wexford in 1988 with Mercadante's *Elisa e Claudio*. Tom Cairns, one of the most promising of the new generation of designers, looks to be another.

One house which has not so far used a director–designer is Glyndebourne. During the '1978 Revolution' Glyndebourne, as so often before, pursued its own course. Independence has ever been the watchword on the Sussex Downs. John Cox was Director of Production there throughout the Seventies and perhaps his greatest coup was to persuade David Hockney to design *The Rake's Progress* for the 1975 season. It was, in the words of Glyndebourne's General Administrator, Brian Dickie, 'An absolutely brilliant bit of casting'. There might have been a few unwanted pauses on the first night, but Hockney held up a mirror to both Hogarth and Stravinsky – not for nothing had one of his earliest set of lithographs been a twentieth-century *Rake's Progress*.

Hockney's success was complete. A *Zauberflöte* followed, also with Cox, and later a triple bill for New York's Met, directed by John Dexter. Parts of this (*Le Rossignol* and *L'Enfant et les Sortilèges*) were later seen at Covent Garden. These were fairy tales for grown-ups, brilliantly coloured and full of quotations from painters contemporary with Stravinsky and Ravel. Glyndebourne had always been adept at linking artists with the stage: Osbert Lancaster had been introduced to Carl Ebert, Hugh Casson to Günther Rennert. Now they had done it again.

While Cox was pursuing his policy of decorated opera in highly individual style – marvellously with Hockney and disastrously with Erté in *Der Rosenkavalier* – Peter Hall was creating his Mozart cycle for Glyndebourne with John Bury. They kept to the three Da Pontes, starting with *Figaro*, going on to *Don Giovanni* (1977) and concluding with *Così fan Tutte* (1978). The style in each case was severe, almost classical, with sombre colours by Glyndebourne standards. The masterpiece was undoubtedly *Don Giovanni*. Not for nothing was that a 'night opera', a piece heavily dependent on disguises, which begins under cover of darkness and ends in hell, followed of course by the famous *envoi*.

Hall and Bury worked on the basis of total fidelity to the text and of never ducking a stage direction – a far cry from what was developing at the Coliseum. Their other tenet was that there should be a strong and unbroken narrative line. This belief proved to be another of the strengths of that *Don Giovanni*. The action moves all over Seville, but Hall and Bury would have considered it a failure to bring down the curtain at any point or to have arias sung in front of the footlights while the scene-shifters did their best – or their worst. So Bury devised a series of 'sliders', scenery which moved silently across the stage so that the opera could progress at the fastest possible pace.

Bury provided two other remarkable sets for Hall, both again were for 'night operas'. One was for *A Midsummer Night's Dream* (Glyndebourne, 1981), a magical evocation of that wood outside Athens, which was quite deliberately made to resemble some of those woods outside Glyndebourne. It was the first Britten opera to be staged there since the performances of *Albert Herring* and *The Rape of Lucretia* in 1947, which had led to a rift between John Christie and Britten. It was generally agreed that the *Dream* should have been seen at Glyndebourne much earlier,

particularly in a staging as persuasive as this. The other Bury set which demonstrated exactly Hall's working methods was the *Salomé* he devised, a glittering and sinister affair, first seen in Los Angeles (1987) and later at Covent Garden. This was convincing enough an answer to those who said that Hall had worked too long with the same designer and that monotony was creeping in.

These artistic marriages are all too easy to form: Pountney with Björnson and later Lazaridis, Moshinsky with O'Brien.... They save time because communication becomes instant and almost intuitive. But, as one designer remarked, the danger is that there arrives a moment when you stop questioning your partner's ideas and start accepting all his or her faults. That is usually the moment for divorce or at least a few major affairs on the side. Hall probably realized this when he turned to John Gunter for his second Britten at Glyndebourne, *Albert Herring*, in 1985. Much of Gunter's operatic experience had come in Germany and Switzerland in the mid-Seventies with Friedrich and, especially, Michael Hampe. The latter had drilled him in the traditional style, productions which were built to please and to last. And although Gunter was quite happy to throw off traditionalism when the occasion demanded it – he has probably never designed a more successful set than that for the National Theatre's *Guys and Dolls* directed by Richard Eyre – *Herring* provided the opportunity to use traditionalism to the full. There, on the Sussex stage, was a slice of Suffolk life, right down to the canned vegetables and sacks of turnips in Albert's greengrocer's.

John Gunter as a designer tends to be demanding and exacting; his attention to detail may at times require funds that have general administrators reaching for their contingency account. But his *Herring* and later his *Falstaff* for Hall – the model ships in Ford's house in the latter tellingly suggested wealth derived from trade – plus his *Porgy and Bess* for Trevor Nunn, with Sue Blane's dazzling costumes, are among the best visual experiences Glyndebourne has provided in the decade. (Intendants are not usually given to praising products of houses other than their own, but one of them said that *Porgy* was so good that it restored his faith in the whole operatic business.) Their obvious rivals are that *Midsummer Night's Dream* and the cool Japanese *Idomeneo* provided by John Napier for Trevor Nunn.

The other major designer helped on his way by Glyndebourne was William Dudley. He had devised a *Billy Budd* in Hamburg back in 1972 for John Dexter, which subsequently went to the Met. The WNO commissioned a small-scale *Barber of Seville* – memories of Mold again! – which became very mock *commedia dell'arte* in William Gaskill's hands. But it was Glyndebourne's 1979 *Entführung* which really moved Dudley into the operatic sphere. It was a mixture of near Eastern glitter and careful architecture – Dudley admits to being a great consumer of art history – and its staying power, despite an erratic production by Peter Wood, meant it was still in the repertoire in 1988.

Dudley followed this with a second *Barber* (Glyndebourne) and a *Tales of Hoffmann* (Covent Garden), both strong on decoration, and a less successful *Don Giovanni* (Covent Garden). And it was he who was given the biggest single operatic commission of any British designer in the decade, *The Ring* at Bayreuth in 1983. Peter Hall was the director. He and William Dudley decided to dispense with all the recent Bayreuth style and go for a totally realistic staging of Wagner; back to the stage directions and no ducking them. So the curtain rose on three naked Rhinemaidens splashing about in real water, while later Siegfried wandered through a tawny forest that might have been devised by Arthur Rackham.

The German critics, some heavily influenced by the fashion for the new brutalism, and cross to find no political statements to grasp, vandalized the production. Certain British and American critics followed suit. Dudley remembers going into a Bayreuth office and being faced with an immense mound of notices, all of them hostile. He turned his back on opera and cancelled an *Otello* for the Vienna State. However, in subsequent seasons, the qualities of that *Ring* began to be recognized. And now the wounds have been partially healed Dudley is to design Verdi's *Ballo in Maschera* for Salzburg in 1989, working with John Schlesinger as he did on *Hoffmann*.

The style of Bury, Gunter and Dudley is essentially narrative. That of the Coliseum in the Eighties, principally under the influence of David Pountney, was one of concept. The single biggest development there was of the one-set conceptual opera, based on the director's view of the work. In part it was a matter of economics: variations on a single structure tend to work out cheaper than a series of separate settings. In part it was the shortcomings backstage which some designers reckoned tied their hands before they even started work. The idea of the one-set opera was not exactly new. David Fielding tried it out for the WNO in 1976 with *Trovatore*, hardly the obvious candidate for the treatment.

The master of the genre became Stefanos Lazaridis, the most protean of the British designers. With the grand opera *Aida* nothing but an uncomfortable memory, he had gone into an experimental period in the early Eighties. One of his major influences was the Russian director, Yuri Lyubimov. Together they produced a successful *Tristan* in Bologna in 1983, which Lazaridis describes as a personal revelation: 'It was like moving house, because I suddenly discovered all the things I did not really need about me on stage.' In Florence, however, they fell flat on their faces with a *Rigoletto* for the Maggio Musicale; Gilda was on a swing amidst a stage filled with crypto-fascist references. Piero Cappuccilli, the veteran baritone, due to sing the title role, walked out before the first night, and *Rigoletto* gave Italy one of its biggest scandals of the decade.

Back in London Lazaridis combined with Graham Vick on a *Madam Butterfly* for the ENO; they dispensed with all the pretty Japanese cherry blossom and instead had Sharpless tramping through the mud and rain to Butterfly's house in a drab quarter of Nagasaki. But it was with Pountney, and again at the Coliseum, that Lazaridis created his three most powerful, but very different 'concept' stagings.

The design of Shostakovitch's *Lady Macbeth of Mtsensk* carried again much of the energetic outrage that had characterized the Norwest season. The bourgeois household of Leskov's original story was turned into a meat warehouse hung with carcases. It won press awards, but just how true the enterprise

119

was to Shostakovitch was somewhat questionable. Humperdinck's *Hansel and Gretel* at Christmas in 1987 also carried elements of nastiness, showing the two children of the title as victims of a deprived post-war childhood. But the imagination of Lazaridis's set – variations on a tatty suburban semi and a public park – tempered the mood. He, though, is proudest of the skyline of filing cabinets which provided the background for Busoni's *Doctor Faust*.

Despite these successes there was a recurrent

119 Albert Herring
Britten

DESIGNER JOHN GUNTER

Glyndebourne, 1985
Director Peter Hall
Lighting David Hersey
Production photograph by Guy Gravett
Jean Rigby (Nancy), Alan Opie (Sid), John Graham-Hall (Albert)

feeling that 'concept production' had run its natural course. This was enforced by the *Traviata* at the Coliseum in the autumn of 1988, which had a cornfield rising in the midst of Violetta's dining table. Lazaridis himself later questioned the visual strait-jacket he was sometimes forced to wear: 'I want to begin to bend the Coliseum. I'm now tired of the single set idea and in future I want the power to decide which operas need a dominant visual image and which multiple ones.'

That was not necessarily the view at Covent Garden where a new *Ring* was beginning. For *Rheingold* in October 1988 there was not even a credit for sets and costumes; instead, in Yuri Lyubimov's production, the attribution 'Design concept Paul Hernon' was used. Hernon's centre stage circle – looking much like a compact disc – seemed old-fashioned, and not the style to take us into the Nineties, when this cycle, now abandoned, was to have been completed. Another one by Götz Friedrich will be imported in its place.

To whom do we look? Among the newest generation three names are beginning to stand out. Richard Hudson's clean-cut, unfussy and imaginative sets, such as that for Scottish Opera's *Candide*, have often been better than the productions for which they have been created. Tom Cairns and Antony McDonald delivered the goods for the joint production by Opera North and the WNO of Berlioz's *The Trojans*. While at the Coliseum, also working with director Tim Albery, they invented a *Billy Budd* that jettisoned the conventional quarter-deck, replacing it with a tilted stage which displayed, in the clearest visual terms, the naval hierarchy at the heart of Britten's opera. The influence of the Peter Stein style at the West Berlin Schaubühne was there for all to see. The decorative school is probably best represented by Bob Crowley.

All have the advantage of working in an atmosphere quite different from that of ten years ago. Opera is currently fashionable, especially among the young. And may it remain so. Part of the reason is that it is drawing in a new theatre-going audience, chiefly because of the efforts of several directors and designers to create drama in opera houses.

The insularity of the Sixties and Seventies is disappearing. The new generation appears to be well informed of what is going on in Europe. Maybe they will be giving us a stronger taste of the Continent, just as Brian McMaster set out to do ten years ago.

The author was arts editor of The Times *from 1970 to 1988, and is now its chief opera critic. From 1963 to 1969 he was arts editor of the* Financial Times. *He is the author of* The Making of an Opera, *and the editor of* Glyndebourne: a Celebration.

120 **Candide**. Bernstein
DESIGNER RICHARD
HUDSON. Costume drawing
for the auto da fe scene.

Scottish Opera, 1988
Directors Jonathan Miller and
John Wells
Lighting Davy Cunningham

120

121A

121A & B **Rigoletto**. Verdi

DESIGNERS PATRICK ROBERTSON and ROSEMARY VERCOE: 'The action is set in Mafia-controlled Little Italy, New York, in the 1950s. Edward Hopper paintings inspired the visual aspect, particularly in Act 3 (*121A*).'

'The drawing (*121B*) is of Rigoletto as chief barman in the "Duke's" hotel headquarters in Act 1, Scene 1. He wore a dark overcoat and hat for the street scenes, a grey work jacket for Act 2.'

English National Opera, 1982
Director Jonathan Miller
Lighting Robert Bryan
Production photograph by Patrick Robertson (121A)
Patricia O'Neill (Gilda), Jonathan Summers (Rigoletto), Jean Rigby (Maddalena), Dennis O'Neill (The Duke)
Costume drawing by Rosemary Vercoe (121B)

121B

123 **Peter Grimes**. Britten

DESIGNERS TIMOTHY O'BRIEN and TAZEENA FIRTH:
'The 19th-century jewel box interior of the Göteborg theatre is,
here, a window on to the sky, sea and shore of Suffolk, where the
people of the Borough and the outsider Grimes struggle with
their fate.'

Storan Theater, Göteborg, 1979
Director Elijah Moshinsky
Lighting Carl Erik Cadier
Production photograph by Timothy O'Brien

122

122 **The Rake's Progress**.
Stravinsky

DESIGNERS TIMOTHY
O'BRIEN and TAZEENA
FIRTH: 'A big opera house,
made to seem a semi-abstract
18th-century chamber theatre,
containing realistic trophies of
acquisition. "Truly there is a
divine balance in nature: a
thousand lose that a thousand
may gain."'

Royal Opera House, 1979
Director Elijah Moshinsky
Lighting Nick Chelton
*Production photograph by Timothy
O'Brien*
Donald Gramm (Nick Shadow),
Robert Tear (Tom Rakewell)

123

124A

124A & B **A Midsummer
Night's Dream**. Britten

DESIGNERS TIMOTHY
O'BRIEN and TAZEENA
FIRTH: 'Shredded
cellophane was suggested for
the pool in this painted image
of a forest *(124A)*. But we
held out for water, since in it
real people got really wet,
stripped of illusions in a world
of illusions.'

'A working man, with
proprieties in place and
wearing Victorian clothes
(124B), takes up "lantern, dog
and bush of thorn" to
represent the moon and gain a
pension of sixpence a day.'

Sydney Opera House, 1978
Director Elijah Moshinsky
Lighting Anthony Everingham
*Model photograph by Timothy
O'Brien*

125A

124B

125B

125A & B **Turandot**. Puccini

DESIGNERS TIMOTHY O'BRIEN and TAZEENA FIRTH: 'Peking lies under the pall of Turandot's vengeful chastity. Fear has driven out morality. The populace are spectators of senseless death. Masks rob them of expression and the mirror sequins of their clothes turn them into chameleons. Calaf submits to the riddles, breaks the spell, and restores light and life to the nightmare city.'

125B   Costume design for the Executioner

Vienna State Opera, 1983
Director Harold Prince
Lighting Ken Billington
Production photograph by Claude Gafner (125A)
Eva Marton (Turandot), José Carreras (Callas)

126

127

126 Il Seraglio. Mozart

DESIGNER TAZEENA FIRTH: 'Sea breezes gently blowing through harem screens, a pool of clear cool water and fresh scented flowers, beautiful women with young children cared for by grandmothers, a loving father – all clear-cut, accepted rules as against Belmonte's western promise of "love till death do us part".'

Storan Theater, Göteborg, 1986
Director David Radok
Lighting Torkel Blomkrist
Production photograph by Ingmar Jernberg
Gritch Fjeldmose (Blonde)

127 The Magic Flute. Mozart

DESIGNER TAZEENA FIRTH: 'One moving curtain – 40 by 28 metres of multi-coloured silk – hanging from an open proscenium-less grid, conjuring up dragons, forest floors, halls and midnight skies, a green birdlike man flying through the air, a silver-faced queen and a golden world where the sun eclipses the moon. Tamino (Act 1): "Am I asleep, am I awake? Is this a dream or reality?"'

Norrlands Operan Umeo, 1987
Director David Radok
Lighting Lars Ostberg
Production photograph by Tazeena Firth
Helge Lannerbäck (Papageno)

128 **Le Grand Macabre**. Ligeti

DESIGNER TIMOTHY O'BRIEN: 'Ligeti's "Beautiful Breughel Land" is the world on the brink of destruction. The motorway is all that remains above the rubbish-silted city. It is a stage for the last act of mankind. Hearses are used for bridal cars. The Chief of Police has the head of a bird.'

English National Opera, 1982
Director Elijah Moshinsky
Lighting Nick Chelton
Production photograph by Timothy O'Brien

129

129 **Samson**. Handel

DESIGNER TIMOTHY O'BRIEN: 'Untamed Samson, eyeless in Gaza, is chained to a cart and paraded before the Philistines and Israelites, set and dressed according to the ideas of Handel's time. His faith delivers his people from captivity.'

Royal Opera House, 1985
Director Elijah Moshinsky
Lighting Nick Chelton
Production photograph by Catherine Ashmore/Dominic Photography
John Vickers (Samson)

130

131A

131B

130 **xes**. Handel

DESIGNER DAVID
FIELDING hite
baroque room and
background a desert vista:
Persepolis meets Vauxhall
Gardens. Xerxes, king of
Persepolis and Persia, in the
presence of his court, and in
the shadow of a topiary
winged god, rewards his
victorious generals after the
battle of Thermopylae.'

English National Opera, 1985
Director Nicholas Hytner
Lighting Paul Pyant
*Production photograph by
Catherine Ashmore*
Ann Murray (Xerxes), Rodney
McCann (Ariodate)

131A&B
Simon Boccanegra. Verdi

DESIGNER DAVID
FIELDING: 'The coast near
Genoa (*131A*) where Amelia
and Gabriele meet. Huge red
walls surround a raked white
floor.'
   'The Palace Council
Chamber (*131B*). On the
throne is Boccanegra, the
Doge; to his right are the
councillors of the people; left,
the nobles. Moments later the
angry mob break in.'

English National Opera, 1986
Director David Alden
Lighting Patricia Collins
*Production photographs by Richard
H. Smith/Dominic Photography*
131A Janice Cairns (Amelia),
Arthur Davies (Gabriele)
131B Jonathan Summers
(Boccanegra), Alan Opie (Paolo)

132

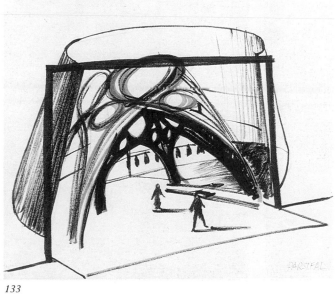

133

132 **Cosi fan Tutte**. Mozart

SET DESIGNER HAYDEN GRIFFIN: 'The approach was to try
and create a theatre-within-a-theatre, to make Mozart's
"chamber" piece work in an opera house holding 5,000 people.'

Metropolitan Opera House, New York, 1982
Director Colin Graham
Costume designer Deirdre Clancy
Lighting Gil Wechsler
Production photograph by Hayden Griffin
Kiri Te Kanawa (Fiordiligi), Maria Ewing (Dorabella)

133 **Parsifal**. Wagner

DESIGNER HAYDEN GRIFFIN: 'This is my initial sketch for
the ruined cathedral structure of the final design.'

Royal Opera House, 1988
Director Bill Bryden
Costumes realized by Jane Moisley
Lighting Rory Dempster

134

136

134 Die Fledermaus. Johann Strauss

DESIGNER PETER RICE: 'The sheet of drawings shows a design concept based on the work of the Secessionist designers in Vienna, and of Mackintosh and Macmurdo at the end of the 19th century. I have used simple linear constructions, with a limited range of colours, beige, amethyst and grey.'

Opera Theater of St Louis, USA, 1983
Director Tom Hawkes
Lighting Peter Kaczorowski

135 The Marriage of Figaro. Mozart

DESIGNER SUE BLANE: 'An acid-yellow standing set. The linen closets of Susanna and Figaro's room (Act 1, shown here) are flown to reveal the Countess's bedroom. In a similar way a library in Act 3 reveals a garden of statues for the final act.'

Welsh National Opera, 1987
Director Giles Havergal
Lighting Durham Marengi
Production photograph by Clive Barda
Catriona Bell (Marcellina), Peter Rose (Dr Bartolo)

135

136 **Christmas Eve**. Rimsky-Korsakoff

DESIGNER SUE BLANE: 'The Ukrainian village of Dikana, shown here, is the setting for the first half of the opera. The second is an elaborate series of tableaux depicting Vakula's flight, with the aid of the devil, through the heavens to the Tsarina's palace in search of a pair of slippers.'

English National Opera, 1988
Director David Pountney
Lighting Chris Ellis
Production photograph by Richard H. Smith/Dominic Photography
Edmund Barham (Vakula, in red), John Connell (Chub, far right)

137 **Porgy and Bess**. Gershwin

COSTUME DESIGNER SUE BLANE.

Costume designs for the women of Catfish Row

Glyndebourne, 1986
Director Trevor Nunn
Set designer John Gunter
Lighting David Hersey

137

109

139

138

138 **Donnerstag aus Licht**. Stockhausen

DESIGNER MARIA BJÖRNSON: 'For Michael's journey across
the world a central staircase was devised enabling him to play the
trumpet walking up and down, while a giroscope globe turned
around the staircase as the whole thing revolved, so giving a still
greater feeling of movement and travel.'

Royal Opera House, 1985
Director Michael Bogdanov
Lighting Chris Ellis
Production photograph by Clive Barda
Markus Stockhausen (Michael)

139 **The Valkyrie**. Wagner

DESIGNER MARIA BJÖRNSON: 'Brünnhilde's rock was set in an enclosed mausoleum with the names of Norse heroes written on black marble walls. The Valkyries' ride was achieved by having them enter as the revolve turned and anti-raked, so that they could appear and disappear. The up-lighting effect was reminiscent of Albert Speer's Nuremberg rallies.

English National Opera, 1983
Director David Pountney
Lighting Nick Chelton
Production photograph by Donald Southern

140 **From the House of the Dead**. Janáček

DESIGNER MARIA BJÖRNSON: 'This set had to trap all its occupants joined in despair, while the piece pounds through to its climax.'

Welsh National Opera, 1982
Director David Pountney
Lighting Chris Ellis
Production photograph by Roger de Wolf
Picture includes from left:
William Mackie, Ralph Hamer, Nigel Douglas, Donald Maxwell, Jeffrey Lawton, Ralph Mason, Graham Clark

140

141

141 Tristan and Isolde.
Wagner

DESIGNER DAVID
HOCKNEY.

Model for Act 1, in which the ship
brings Isolde from Ireland to
Cornwall. The ship is decorated
with Saxon and Celtic patterns.

Los Angeles Music Center Opera,
1987
Director Jonathan Miller
Lighting David Hockney
*Model photograph copyright David
Hockney*

142

142 Le Rossignol.
Stravinsky

DESIGNER DAVID
HOCKNEY: '. . . three
ambassadors from the
Emperor of Japan arrive with
a present – a mechanical
nightingale. It isn't a Sony or a
Panasonic, it's old-fashioned
clockwork. They open the box
and wind it up . . . it sings
away. Everyone thinks it's
quite lovely, but it's actually
garish and hideous compared
to the real one . . . and of
course it always sings the same
way.'

Metropolitan Opera House, New
York, 1981
Director John Dexter
Lighting Gil Wechsler
*Photograph copyright David
Hockney*

143

143 The Mikado. Sullivan

DESIGNER TIM GOODCHILD:
'Costumes were a mix of
traditional Japanese with
Victorian and modern British.
For instance, the three little
maids were geishas as well as
St Trinian's schoolgirls; the
Gentlemen of Japan (drawing)
were city businessmen with
"Times" fans, rolled
umbrellas, pin-striped
kimonos, wing collars and ties,
and red carnation buttonholes.
This mix also followed
through into the set design.'

New Sadler's Wells Opera
Company, 1983
Director Christopher Renshaw
Lighting Steven Watson

144 Alceste. Gluck

DESIGNER ROGER BUTLIN:
'The production used
elements of classical imagery
and line to achieve a state of
ritual. These costumes for
Alceste were black and red
(Act 1), cream and gold (Act 2)
and, in Act 3, shrouds of grey.'

Kentucky Opera, 1982
Director Lilian Hope
Lighting Richard Riddell

144

145

146

145 **Cosi fan Tutte**. Mozart

DESIGNER JOHN BURY: 'A traditional setting whose virtue lay in the ability to provide all the required changes of locale without stopping the action – or the music. The secret lay in the effortlessly sliding walls, and Glyndebourne's nimble "supers".'

Glyndebourne, 1978
Director Peter Hall
Lighting John Bury
Production photograph by Guy Gravett of the 1984 revival
Standing, from left: Claudio Desderi (Don Alfonso), Delores Ziegler (Dorabella), Carol Vaness (Fiordiligi), Jane Berbié (Despina). On ground: J Patrick Raftery (Guglielmo), Ryland Davies (Ferrando)

146 **The Bartered Bride**. Smetana

DESIGNER JOHN BURY: 'This is Ludmilla, Marenka's mum, entertaining at the picnic. The period was moved into the early Twenties, shortly after the First World War and the break-up of the Austro-Hungarian Empire. This enabled the use of traditional peasant costume (as Sunday best) for the young, to be set against the real world of an economically struggling peasantry.'

English National Opera, 1985
Director Elijah Moshinsky
Lighting Nick Chelton
Costume drawing by Elizabeth Bury

147 **A Midsummer Night's Dream**. Britten

DESIGNER JOHN BURY: 'The Forest is alive – a group of twelve tree-actors, bush-actors and bough-actors respond emotionally and physically to the music, the lovers, and the night. Mirrored walls and a mirrored floor reinforce a constantly reforming image. All is black until a golden sun rises into a green land.'

Glyndebourne, 1981
Director Peter Hall
Lighting John Bury
Production photograph by Guy Gravett of the 1984 revival
Elizabeth Gale (Tytania)

147

114

148 **Salomé**. Richard Strauss

DESIGNER JOHN BURY: 'The use of a painted gauze, front and rear projections, figured mirror walls and floor, and a floating moon create a seamless sequence of visual transformations. Here Salomé is about to discard the seventh veil.'

Royal Opera House, 1988
Director Peter Hall
Lighting John Bury
Production photograph by Catherine Ashmore/Dominic Photography
Maria Ewing (Salomé)

148

149 **The Magic Flute**.
Mozart

DESIGNER NIGEL PRABHAVALKAR: 'This is Tamino being saved by a monster (Act 1). But without the resources to create one frightening enough, Richard Jones and I translated this moment into an adolescent boy's nightmare – a predatory fire-breathing woman.'

Cambridge Arts Theatre, 1987
Director Richard Jones
Lighting Nigel Prabhavalkar and Nick Safford
Production photograph by 'Requiem to Because'
Mark Padmore (Tamino)

150 **L'Elisir d'Amore**.
Donizetti

DESIGNER GERARD HOWLAND: 'This is the design/painting I did for the setting of the opera, which I wanted to be a bright practical landscape, provincial, Italian, and ideal for devotion to the fair sex.'

Städtische Bühnen Dortmund, 1983
Director Gerlinde Fulle
Lighting Wolfgang Rettig

149

150

151 **Fidelio**. Beethoven

DESIGNER PETER MUMFORD: 'The Prisoners' Chorus in Act 1. I set the opera in its own time rather than in a modern context, the story taking place in a crumbling neo-classical mausoleum in post-revolutionary France. A time jump at the end introduced a contemporary chorus, dressed rather like a UN delegation, who examine the evidence of the performance and comment on it.'

Opera North, 1988
Director Michael McCarthy
Lighting Peter Mumford
Production photograph by Hanson
Centre: Janice Cairns (Leonora)

151

152 **Semele**. Handel

COSTUME DESIGNER DAVID WALKER: 'The formal conventions of 18th-century *opera seria* and allegorical paintings of the time were used loosely as references; both seemed implicit in the work.'

Costume designs for Somnus and Pasythae

Royal Opera House, 1982
Director John Copley
Set designer Henry Bardon
Lighting Robert Bryan

152

153A

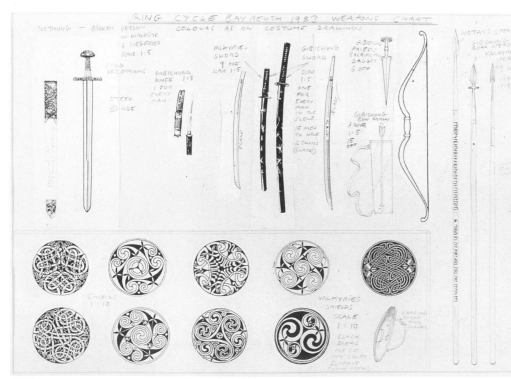

153B

153A–D The Ring. Wagner

DESIGNER WILLIAM DUDLEY: 'The brief Peter Hall gave me was to follow Wagner's own stage instructions, however difficult. He wanted a direct naiveté, showing nature beginning in a state of grace. For the illusion of the bottom of the Rhine, the Rhine maidens swam naked in a 50-foot tank (*153C*) reflected vertically in a suspended mirror.'

153A   Drawing for the hall of the Gibichungs
153B   References for weapons and shields
153C   Das Rheingold (Act 1)
153D   Design for Das Rheingold (Act 1)

Bayreuth, 1983
Director Peter Hall
Lighting Manfred Voss
Production photograph by Roger Wood
(*153A*, *B* and *D* Collection Robert Pennant-Jones)

153C

153D

154 **La Traviata**. Verdi

DESIGNER JOHN GUNTER: 'The design was intended to show the seamy underbelly of a rich decadent society being counted away by the tick of clocks.'

Glyndebourne, 1987
Director Peter Hall
Lighting David Hersey
Production photograph by Guy Gravett

155 **Porgy and Bess**. Gershwin

SET DESIGNER JOHN GUNTER: 'Trevor Nunn and I agreed that the design should reflect the teeming world of this black community in the late 18th-century colonial house they have taken over, as in DuBose Heyward's novel *Porgy* which Gershwin used for the basis of his opera.'

Glyndebourne, 1986
Director Trevor Nunn
Costume designer Sue Blane
Lighting David Hersey
Model photograph by Guy Gravett

154

156

156 **Faust**. Gounod

SET DESIGNER JOHN GUNTER: 'Ian Judge went back to the original score and libretto to simplify the piece. The design had to reflect this and keep the action going swiftly by simple statements, to ease the flow of the scenes.'

English National Opera, 1985
Director Ian Judge
Costume designer Deirdre Clancy
Lighting Steven Watson
Production photograph by Donald Southern

155

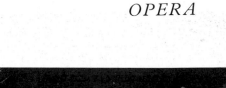

158

158   Turandot. Puccini

DESIGNER SALLY JACOBS: 'The dark interior of a theatre-on-stage allowed the story to be told in a series of theatrical tableaux. The audience is continued around the stage where it becomes a Chinese chorus/audience, watching and reacting to the events.'

Royal Opera House, 1984
Director Andrei Serban
Lighting F. Mitchell Dana
Choreographer Kate Flatt
Production photograph by Zoë Dominic

157   Fidelio. Beethoven

DESIGNER SALLY JACOBS: 'The imagery was taken from engravings, expressing the opera's themes – redemption, freedom, the soul's release from earthly suffering. The picture shows the overture elements, all enclosed in one vast "dungeon", which later breaks open as Leonora rescues Florestan and sunlight streams in.'

Royal Opera House, 1986
Director Andrei Serban
Lighting Robert Ryan
Production photograph by Group Three Photography
Elizabeth Connell (Leonora)

157

159 **Ariadne auf Naxos**.　Richard Strauss

COSTUME DESIGNER DEIRDRE CLANCY: 'This costume was part of a group of commedia characters. My idea was that they should be magical and traditional images filtered through late 19th-century eyes.'

English National Opera, 1981
Director Jeremy James Taylor
Set designer Douglas Heap
Lighting Mark Henderson

160 **Macbeth**. Verdi

COSTUME DESIGNER DEIRDRE CLANCY: 'The witches were conceived as real if malevolent women, possessed of some genuine psychic powers. Macbeth finds them believable, so the audience should as well.'

Opera North, 1987
Director Ian Judge
Set designer John Gunter
Lighting Paul Pyant

160

161 **L'Elisir d'Amore**. Donizetti

DESIGNER ROBIN DON: 'Many 19th-century operas can benefit from a contemporary interpretation. This little gem seemed perfectly fine set in a style evocative of its own period. Dr Dulcamara's arrival by balloon was an unexpected novelty.'

Opera Northern Ireland, 1982
Director Christopher Renshaw
Lighting Mick Hughes
Production photograph by Robin Don

162 **Tamerlano**. Handel

DESIGNER ROBIN DON: 'The decorative fussiness often associated with 18th-century opera seemed wrong for the brutal story. This Act 1 photograph shows the ruins of the burnt out city under repair: the vanquished sultan is encaged while the Tartar conqueror conducts his relentless ambitions. Rebuilding is completed by the finale.'

Opéra de Lyon, 1984
Director Anthony Besch
Lighting Philippe Arlaud
Production photograph by Robin Don

159

161

163

163 The Midsummer Marriage. Tippett

DESIGNER ROBIN DON:
'There are shadows, dangers and a death in the opera, but its main song is of fruitfulness and joy. The designs attempted to echo a phrase from Tippett's definition of a modern composer's task: "To create . . . in an age of mediocrity and shattered dreams, images of abounding, generous, exuberant beauty".'

San Francisco Opera, 1983
Director John Copley
Lighting Thomas Munn
Production photograph by Ron Scherl

164A

164B

164A&B   **The Magic Flute**. Mozart

DESIGNER RUSSELL CRAIG: 'The black ceiling of the Queen of the Night becomes the white floor of Sarastro's kingdom. The large organ that dominates this world (*164B*) is initially masked by a paper screen representing the three temples (*164A*). The animals appear slowly, tearing their way through it. The slaves destroy it further.'

Opera North, 1984
Director Graham Vick
Lighting Nick Chelton
Production photographs by James Joseph
164A   Laurence Dale (Tamino)
164B   Alan Watt (Papageno), Jane Leslie Mackenzie (Pamina)

166 **Montag aus Licht**. Stockhausen

SET DESIGNER CHRIS DYER: 'The figure Eva represents Mother Earth. She was woken, cleaned, prepared for life-giving, gave life, and then succumbed to the force of Nature which she had created.'

La Scala, Milan, 1988
Director Michael Bogdanov
Costume designer Mark Thompson
Lighting Gianni Mantovanini
Production photograph by Chris Dyer
Suzanne Stephens (Coeur de Basset)

165

165 **Billy Budd**. Britten

DESIGNER CHRIS DYER: 'Steel and glass images of prison in the shape of a warship of Nelson's time, encased in an enormous globe: claustrophobia and threatened sexuality in a harsh and unsympathetic environment.'

Scottish Opera, 1987
Director Graham Vick
Lighting Nick Chelton
Production photograph by Eric Thorburn
Philip Langridge (Captain) Mark Tinkler (Billy Budd, kneeling)

166

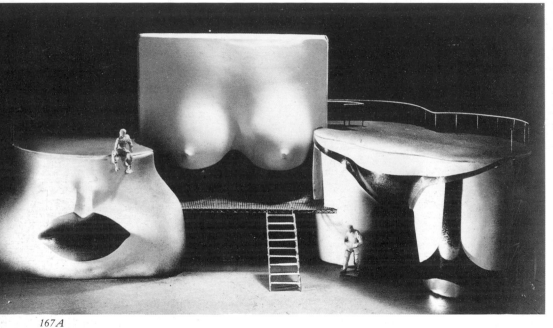

167A

167A & B **Les Soldats**. Zimmermann

SET DESIGNER RALPH KOLTAI: 'Ken Russell requested four acting areas. The model photograph (*167A*) shows a surreal composition – a metaphor for a story essentially about the degradation of women by men. The four acting areas are top left, top right, linking gantry centre, and stage floor. The production photograph (*167B*) shows the ability to "transform" these areas with two very powerful projectors (4kw and 67cm lenses) positioned at the rear of the stalls. Directed on the centre section (breasts), the projections become the dominant image.'

Opéra de Lyon, 1983
Director Ken Russell
Costume designer Annena Stubbs
Lighting Nick Chelton
Model and production photographs by Ralph Koltai

167B

126

168

170

168 **Tosca**. Puccini

DESIGNER STEFANOS LAZARIDIS: 'The period was updated to the Nazi occupation of Rome, and produced as a *film noir*. The set was a permanent structure within which various objects specified the locale of each act.'

Maggio Musicale, Florence, 1986
(co-production with the English National Opera)
Director Jonathan Miller
Lighting Nick Chelton
Model photograph of Act 3 by Clive Barda

169 **Oedipus Rex**. Stravinsky

DESIGNER STEFANOS LAZARIDIS: 'Stravinsky perfectly expressed my response to the opera: "... the individual as the victim of circumstances is made far more starkly effective by this static presentation. Crossroads are not personal but geometrical, and the geometry of tragedy, the inevitable intersecting of lines, is what concerned me".'

Opera North, 1987
Director Stefanos Lazaridis with Michael Hunt (original production Patrick Libby, 1981)
Lighting Davy Cunningham with Stefanos Lazaridis
Production photograph by Phil Cutts
Antony Roden (Oedipus)

169

170 **Lady Macbeth of Mtsensk**. Shostakovich

DESIGNER STEFANOS LAZARIDIS: 'The Prison Scene. We updated the opera to the time of Stalin's purges. The rotating set was made out of metal and paper.'

English National Opera, 1987
Director David Pountney
Lighting Paul Pyant
Model photograph by Clive Barda

171 **Madam Butterfly**. Puccini

DESIGNER STEFANOS LAZARIDIS.

Model for Act 2, the humming chorus

English National Opera, 1984
Director Graham Vick
Lighting Matthew Richardson
Model photograph by Clive Barda

171

172 **Rusalka**. Dvořák

DESIGNER STEFANOS LAZARIDIS.

Model for Act 3

English National Opera, 1983
Director David Pountney
Lighting Nick Chelton
Model photograph by Clive Barda

173A&B **The Midsummer Marriage**. Tippett

SET DESIGNER STEFANOS LAZARIDIS: 'The opera charts the symbolic progress of the union of opposites, the Apollonian and the Dionisiac, purged in the fires of midsummer ritual. The libretto, both simple and complex, draws on an eclectic storehouse of references and allusions. The setting provided a similarly playful, symbolic landscape for the simultaneously naïve and philosophical journey.'

173A   The transfiguration of Mark and Jenifer
173B   The fire dance

English National Opera, 1985
Director David Pountney
Costume designer Sally Gardner
Lighting Nick Chelton
Model photographs by Zoë Dominic

174A&B **Orlando**. Handel

DESIGNER ANTONY McDONALD: 'One of Handel's magic operas, so it was important to conjure up a surreal world that could be at times interior, exterior, hospital, hotel, prison, and where people were not restricted to any particular period. As in a dream, each moment was played out for its own emotional value.'

Scottish Opera, 1984
Director Christopher Fettes
Lighting Paul Pyant
Production photographs by Eric Thorburn
174A   Timothy Wilson (Medoro), Eiddwen Harrhy (Angelica)
174B   James Bowman (Orlando, on bed)

174A

174B

B

131

175A

175B

175A&B   **Clemenza di Tito**. Mozart

DESIGNER NICHOLAS GEORGIADIS: 'This *opera seria* appears to reflect more the Enlightenment's obsession with ancient Rome than any historical reconstruction of the Rome of the Caesars. Therefore fragments of Roman statuary, as in an 18th-century *cabinet d'antiquités*, seemed a relevant approach.'

175A   Costume drawing for Sesto

Aix-en-Provence, 1988
Director Michael Cacoyannis
Lighting Hans Äke Sjöquist
Model photograph by Richard Holttum (175B)

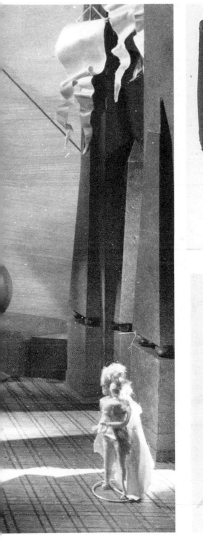

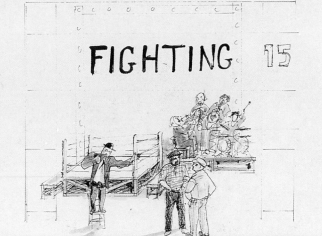

176A–D

176A–D **The Rise and Fall of the City of Mahagonny**. Weill

DESIGNER JOCELYN HERBERT.

Action drawings for scene in Act 2

Metropolitan Opera House, New York, 1979
Director John Dexter
Lighting Gil Wechsler

177A

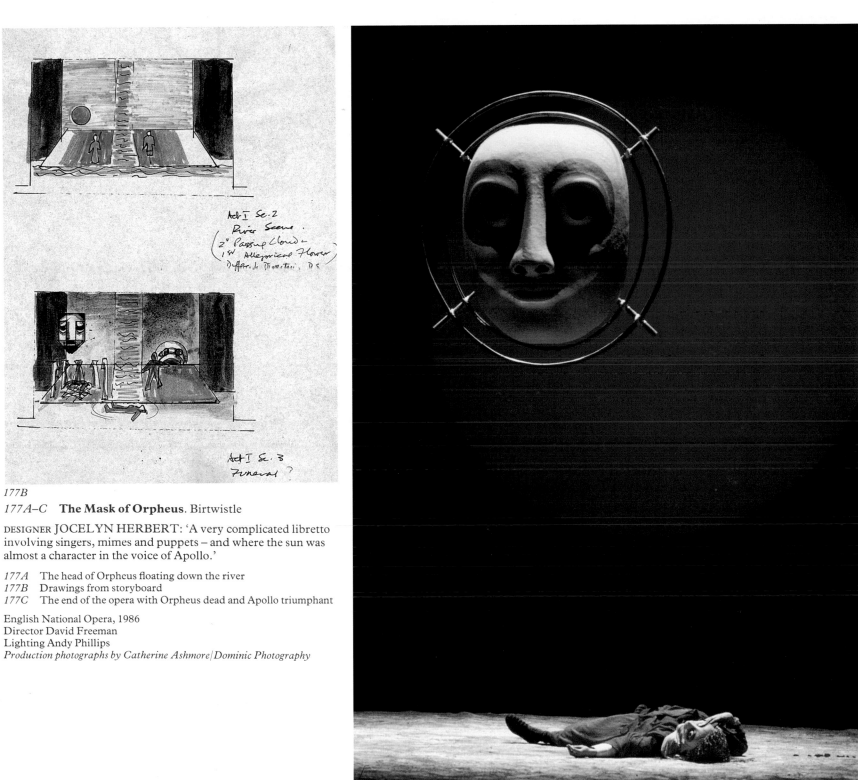

177B

177A–C **The Mask of Orpheus**. Birtwistle

DESIGNER JOCELYN HERBERT: 'A very complicated libretto involving singers, mimes and puppets – and where the sun was almost a character in the voice of Apollo.'

177A   The head of Orpheus floating down the river
177B   Drawings from storyboard
177C   The end of the opera with Orpheus dead and Apollo triumphant

English National Opera, 1986
Director David Freeman
Lighting Andy Phillips
Production photographs by Catherine Ashmore/Dominic Photography

177C

178

178 **Falstaff**. Verdi

DESIGNER PAUL BROWN: 'Graham Vick wanted a Falstaff of
Benny Hill proportions, not a sad introspective fatty. Characters
were forced to clamber and teeter over a perilously raked stage,
riddled with a geometric arrangement of trap-doors and pitfalls.
Costumes proclaimed the vanities and vulgarities of the
bourgeoisie.'

Costume designs for Mistress Quickly and Bardolfo

National tour, 1987
Director Graham Vick
Lighting Jan Sendor

179

179 **Lear**. Reiman

COSTUME DESIGNER PRISCILLA TRUETT: 'John Cox found
many parallels in the characters' situations with those of the
afflicted persons in the triptychs of the painter Max Beckman.
The small cast, and the intimacy of the theatre, enabled me to
individualize the singers more than is usual in opera.'

Costume drawing for The Fool

Nuremberg Musiktheater, 1982
Director John Cox
Set designer John Gunter
Lighting Rudolf Tischer

180A&B Carmen. Bizet

DESIGNER NIGEL LOWERY:
'Act 1 (*180A*) showed an urban Mediterranean society, against which Carmen could react. The tavern scene (*180B*) was a tiny room containing the whole chorus and dancers, squeezed. A picture of mountains hints at the world of the next act, and glows at certain moments.'

Opera North, 1987
Director Richard Jones
Lighting Davy Cunningham
Production photographs by Hanson
180A John Hall (Zuniga)
180B Linda McLeod
(Mercedes, far left), Cynthia
Buchan (Carmen, far right), Juliet
Booth (Frascita, right)

180A

180B

181A

181B

181A&B **Silverlake**. Weill

DESIGNER LEZ BROTHERSTON: 'The design was an attempt to allow the strata of German pre-war society to be played on different levels, height indicating achievement. Inhabitants of the Silverlake shanty town lived in mud and water whilst the bourgeoisie occupied the bridges, the upper levels.'

181B   Costume drawing for Severin

Camden Festival, 1987
Director John Eaton
Lighting John Waterhouse
Model photograph by Lez Brotherston (181A)

182

182 **Jcnůfa**. Janáčck

DESIGNER PAUL HERNON: 'We decided to avoid the folkloric; to have all the scenic elements present from the beginning, and to introduce nothing new except for leaves and snow, strewn across the stage to indicate the passing of the three seasons.'

Royal Opera House, 1986
Director Yuri Lyubimov
Lighting Paul Hernon and Robert Bryan
Production photograph by Catherine Ashmore/Dominic Photography
From left: Ashley Putnam (Jenůfa), Elizabeth Bainbridge (Grandmother Buryja), Linda Kitchen (Jano)

183 **Les Soldats**. Zimmermann

COSTUME DESIGNER ANNENA STUBBS: 'This is the God of War as a female deity, leather-clad in night-club strip, to emphasize both the sexual glamour and the degradation of war in a mainly masculine society with macho ideals.'

Opéra de Lyon, 1983
Director Ken Russell
Set designer Ralph Koltai
Lighting Nick Chelton

183

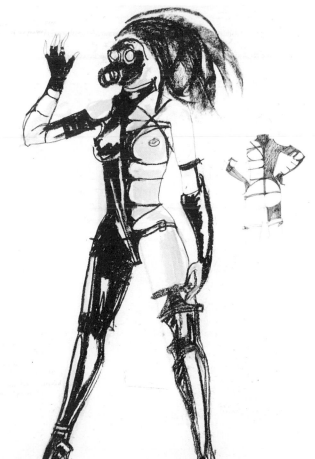

184A

184A&B **Orpheus in the Underworld**. Offenbach

DESIGNER GERALD SCARFE: 'The cloth (*184A*) was designed as a setting for Orpheus's violin solo. He tears off his dull clothes to reveal underneath a spangled, glittering white suit. The backcloth falls into place and shows the audience as Orpheus would like to imagine them – applauding wildly. The truth is he's a rather awful violinist, as Euridice knows only too well . . .'

'Orpheus is accused (*184B*) – by Thatcherite public opinion and two large threatening fingers from above.'

English National Opera, 1985
Director David Pountney
Lighting Nick Chelton
Production photographs by Zoë Dominic (184A) and Chris Davies (184B)
184A   Stuart Kale (Orpheus), Nan Christie (Euridice)
184B   Sally Burgess (Public Opinion)

184B

185

185 **Samson et Dalila**. Saint-Saëns

DESIGNER TOM CAIRNS: 'The Temple of Dagon, scene of the bacchanal, and where the Philistines' orgiastic worship is held. In the opera's last moments Samson destroys the temple. The golden painting at the back is revealed further by opening up the walls and ceiling to show real pillars which collapse on the crowd as the curtain falls.'

Bregenzer Festspiele, Austria, 1988
Director Steven Pimlott
Lighting Davy Cunningham
Production photograph courtesy of Bregenzer Festspiele

186A

186B

186A&B **Akhnaten**. Glass

DESIGNER DAVID ROGER: 'Vital to the mystery surrounding
Akhnaten was his hermaphroditic appearance (*186A*), and in
sessions of several hours a complete body make-up was recreated
every night by Christopher Tucker.'

  'We wanted to convey the vastness of the Egyptian landscape
by opening the Coliseum proscenium to its widest and giving the
performers as much space as possible. Having few scenic points
of reference, it was possible to be free with scale, treating the
stage as a distant city built of sand, or an archeological site of
today, or the edge of the world touched by a huge sun (*186B*).'

English National Opera, 1986
Director David Freeman
Lighting Richard Riddell
Production photographs by Donald Southern
186A   Christopher Robson (Akhnaten)
186B   Sally Burgess (Nefertiti, centre right)

142

187

187 **A Midsummer Night's Dream**. Britten

DESIGNER JOHN MACFARLANE: 'Oberon manipulates the set (three enormous black walls) to surround the lovers with chaos, darkness and night creatures, creating a claustrophobic box. Tytania's grotesque baroque court glides, milky and transparent. Puck yells and shrieks, a demonic punk. Hippolyta – seen here – and the Athenian court are powerless Elizabethan puppets of white crumpled paper.'

Costume drawing for Hippolyta (Collection John Sims)

Cologne Opera House, 1988
Director Willy Decker
Lighting Hans Tolsteder

188

188   **The Magic Flute**.
Mozart

DESIGNER BOB CROWLEY:
'The white curved wall
cracked open to allow Tamino
and Pamina's various
experiences to intrude upon
the empty space of the set.'

English National Opera, 1988
Director Nicholas Hytner
Lighting Nick Chelton
*Production photograph by
Antony Waterman*

189

189   **The King Goes Forth
to France**. Sallinen

DESIGNER BOB CROWLEY:
'The cannon was used by the
invading English king to
devastate the French
countryside (literally, for it
rolled over fields of poppies);
to take part in the battle of
Crecy; and to lay siege to the
town of Calais.'

Royal Opera House, 1986
Director Nicholas Hytner
Lighting Robert Bryan
*Production photograph by
Catherine Ashmore*
Mikael Melbye (the King)

190   **Billy Budd**. Britten

DESIGNERS TOM CAIRNS
& ANTONY McDONALD:
'We decided against a
naturalistic setting usually
associated with this opera in
favour of a more abstract and
universal one. The confined
space of the cabins, revealed
beneath the stage rake,
expressed the claustrophobia
below decks.'

English National Opera, 1988
Director Tim Albery
Lighting Davy Cunningham
*Production photograph by
Clive Barda*

191 **The Midsummer Marriage**. Tippett

DESIGNERS TOM CAIRNS & ANTONY McDONALD: 'Here (in contrast to the way we approached *Billy Budd*) we brought a more realistic style to an abstract piece and set it in the 1950s when it was written. The picture shows the arrival of Mme Sosostris the fortune-teller at Mark and Jenifer's wedding.'

Opera North, 1985
Director Tim Albery
Lighting Charles Paton
Production photograph by Picture House Ltd
Peter Jeffes (Jack), Philip Joll (King Fisher), Penelope Walker (Mme Sosostris)

191

190

193A

193A&B **A Night at the Chinese Opera**. Judith Weir

DESIGNER RICHARD HUDSON: 'The simple white box set played an important part in the story. Windows opened to show the sky outside, the back wall cracked open to reveal the invading Mongolians and split apart to become the mountains. Part of the rake lifted up for the digging of canals, and a topographical model ascended through the floor.'

Kent Opera, 1987
Director Richard Jones
Lighting Nick Chelton
Production photographs by Catherine Ashmore
193A Jonathan Best (Mongolian soldier), Michael Chance (Military Governor), Tomos Ellis (Nightwatchman)
193B Gwion Thomas (Chao Lin), David Johnston (Mountain dweller)

193B

192 **Mignon**.
Ambroise Thomas

DESIGNER RICHARD HUDSON: 'The second act ended with the burning down of the theatre; the entire set collapsed and the chorus ran panic-stricken up and down the aisles. This is a costume design for the ballerinas whose tutus have caught fire.'

Wexford Festival, 1986
Director Richard Jones
Lighting John Waterhouse

192

194A & B **Manon**. Massenet

DESIGNER RICHARD HUDSON: 'The gambling scene was dressed in red except for the sharpers, who wore exaggeratedly flared black coats, tricorns with masks, and cravats and sleeve-frills made of stuffed white gloves which glowed menacingly in the ultra-violet lighting.'
(caption continued below)

194A

194B

DESIGNER RICHARD HUDSON: 'The set for the Cours-la-Reine scene. The rake was very steep and in sharp perspective. Exhibits of curiosities such as the giant memento-mori and stuffed rhinoceros were suspended from the flies.'

Royal Northern College of Music, 1987 (Opera North, 1989)
Director Richard Jones
Lighting Davy Cunningham
Model photograph by Peter Davison

195A

195B

195C

'THE GREAT BRITISH MUSICAL'

TREVOR NUNN

'We are the Cinderellas of the theatre', a designer friend once complained to me. 'We do a lot of the work but we don't get invited to the ball.' Certainly the British have an ambivalent reaction to design that you do not find in, say, Germany, France or Italy; perhaps this is because of a tradition in our performing arts of puritan constraints, from which we have never fully broken free. Whatever the reason is, there can surely be little doubt that the work of our leading designers is undervalued.

If there had been a book about British theatre design for the decade 1968 to 1978, it is unlikely that it would have included a separate section on the British musical. By 1970 Lloyd Webber and Rice had made it clear to anyone interested that the musical theatre had changed irrevocably because of *Jesus Christ Superstar*, but most commentators would have predicted that writers of American musicals would have adapted accordingly and that London would continue to play host to Broadway entertainments crossing the Atlantic with their productions, sets, costumes and leading players intact.

Explanations as to why the reverse has happened, with the traffic beginning to flow in the opposite direction, are easy to come by in retrospect. The American commercial theatre, which really means the New York commercial theatre, has long been dominated not by creative artists, but by producers and theatre owners attempting to follow published critical taste rather than challenge and redefine it. The New York critics and theatre journalists, as if obeying policy decisions voted

195A–C **Cats**. Music Andrew Lloyd Webber. Text T. S. Eliot

DESIGNER JOHN NAPIER: 'The most difficult thing was inventing a world for cats that wasn't cosy and pantomimic, but more Eliot-like, a deserted, lonely wasteground where they could meet and have some kind of ritual. The scale I worked to was $3\frac{1}{2}$ times life-size, because we wanted the audience to see that world through the cats' own eyes.'

Costume designs for Macavity (*195B*) and Growltiger (*195C*)

New London Theatre, 1981
Director Trevor Nunn
Lighting David Hersey
195A   Production photograph by John Napier
The company

149

196A

upon at some clandestine annual conference, are implacably opposed to post-revolutionary popular music, which is to say everything influenced by Elvis Presley and the Beatles onwards. Instead, they are literally entranced by the tradition of the Broadway musical and the nostalgic romance of the acoustic pit orchestra of the Thirties, Forties and Fifties even though it is clear that much of this expression is archaic, and has no contemporary audience other than the escapists in retreat from the world we live in.

Trapped between these twin arms of the producer and critic nutcracker are a host of original and talented American writers and composers, discouraged into repeating endless variations of the old musical play format if they are to get their work staged. Much worse, there has been (with little exception) a serious breakdown of what was once a vital connection between theatre music and the record business. Time was when international recording artists looked to the latest Broadway offerings for their material so that the pop and dance-hall market was in part experiencing the more specialized world of music theatre. But with the arrival of rock n' roll, a gulf between the two publics opened up, a gulf only rarely bridged, most notably and successfully by Lloyd Webber and Rice. Indeed it is now so wide that a show arriving on Broadway containing songs that have achieved international record success immediately arouses suspicion and invites contempt, because supposedly it cannot have been aimed at the theatre. There has also been a concomitant narrowing in the range of subject matter, with writers returning to 'backstage' and 'showbusiness' stories in order to justify the recycling of pastiche musical styles.

It is surely unlikely that this situation will long continue. Be warned that the last decade – one in which British musicals arrived on Broadway with their original productions, sets, costumes and in some cases even leading players intact – may never be repeated. The many musical productions of British origin making the

196A&B **Les Misérables**. Alain Boublil and Claude-Michel Schönberg from Victor Hugo's novel. Lyrics Herbert Kretzmer. Music Claude-Michel Schönberg

DESIGNER JOHN NAPIER: 'My starting point was the centre of the play's biggest moment, the barricade (*196A*). Once that was solved everything else fell into place. The barricade could split, lift, and revolve, and was a mass of *objets trouvés* which the actors picked up from time to time and used.'

COSTUME DESIGNER ANDREANE NEOFITOU: 'We wanted the design to have absolute reality. The clothes also had to allow quick changes – many actors played more than one part. Safety and mobility were big factors too, for most of the cast had to be able to clamber over the enormous barricade structure in the setting.'

196B Costume drawing for M. and Mme Thenardier

Royal Shakespeare Company, 1985
Adapted and directed by Trevor Nunn and John Caird
Lighting David Hersey
Production photograph by Chris Davies (196A)

197A

197B

197C

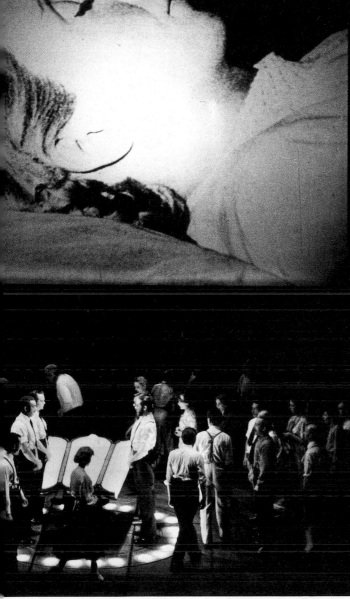

translatlantic journey during those ten years were extraordinarily diverse, with a completely bizarre range of subject matter: the rise and fall of an Argentinian dictator; the annual eisteddfod of a tribe of street cats; the adaptation of a nineteenth-century plea for justice with over twenty on-stage deaths; the dreamlife of a train set; East–West brinkmanship at a chess championship; and (marginally more part of the Broadway world picture) murder, obsession, violence and disfigurement in the Paris Opera House.

Of those inventions which (as yet) have stayed at home, there were musical adaptations of the mutiny on board HMS Bounty; a spacecraft journey to a supreme court trial somewhere in another galaxy; scenes of Cumbrian life before, during and after the Great War; the British opium trade hiding under the skirts of Victoria's Empire; newspaper pride and prejudice in corrupt Chicago; and the optimistic travels of a fourteenth-century minstrel in search of Richard Coeur de Lion. Or in other words, comical, historical, tragical, pastoral, you name it.

Together with this expansion of the boundaries of subject and an exuberant readiness to write for all the electrically energized resources of the recording studio, Lloyd Webber, Rice and their contemporaries have also made the operatic form the rule and the play-with-music form the exception. Accordingly their demands have become more cinematic: they have systematically overturned the notions of song and dance structure (front cloth entertainment in order to mask scene-changing, songs to illustrate scenes, and scenes to justify songs), and removed all awareness of compartmentalized and defined contributions by book writers and choreographers.

Great British designers, from Inigo Jones onwards, seem always to have sensed scope and challenge in stage musical works. With the exception of the unique and

197A–D **Evita**. Music Andrew Lloyd Webber. Book and lyrics Tim Rice

DESIGNERS TIMOTHY O'BRIEN and TAZEENA FIRTH: 'The musical described, but did not celebrate, the rise of Eva Duarte. She became Evita Peron, the darling of the masses of Argentina. Starting bad Hollywood, she ended up good Hollywood (*197A*).'

'It was the purpose of the front cloth, and the paintings in the auditorium (*197B*) to show Argentine society before, during and after the events on stage and to remind us that "when the people contend for their liberty, they seldom get anything by their victory but new masters".'

'Santa Evita's icon floats above the relic of her body (*197C*), which will be stolen and kept hidden for seventeen years.'

'Parody military men, blind puppets, thrashing the air (*197D*), when their power is threatened.'

Prince Edward Theatre, London, 1978
Director Harold Prince
Lighting David Hersey
Production photograph by Tazeena Firth (197A)
Elaine Page (Evita), Susannah Fellows (Maid)
Photograph by John Hewitt (197B) of Peter Parr painting an auditorium mural
Production photograph by Zoë Dominic (197C)
The company
Production photograph by Donald Cooper (197D)
The men's chorus

197D

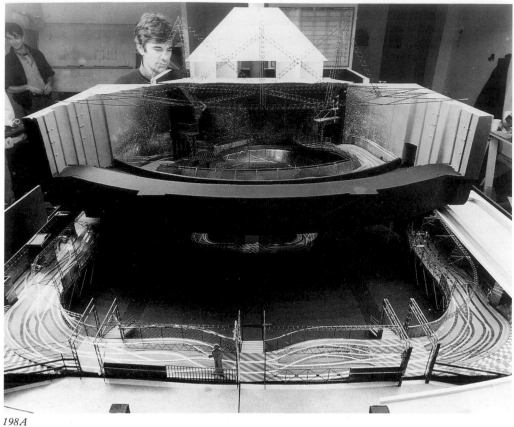

198A

198B

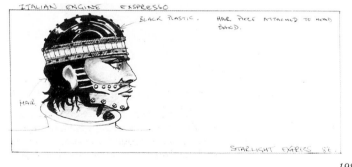

ITALIAN ENGINE ESPRESSO

BLACK PLASTIC. HAIR PIECE ATTACHED TO HEAD BAND.

HAIR

STARLIGHT EXPRESS 86

RUSSIAN ENGINE TURNOFF

FALSE HAIR OR EAR

LENINGR

STARLIGHT EXPRESS 86

198C

FRENCH ENGINE BOBO

BERET.

FALSE PRICES.

STARLIGHT EXPRESS 86

JAPANESE ENGINE YOSHIMOTO

HEADRESS ONLY

STARLIGHT EXPRESS 86

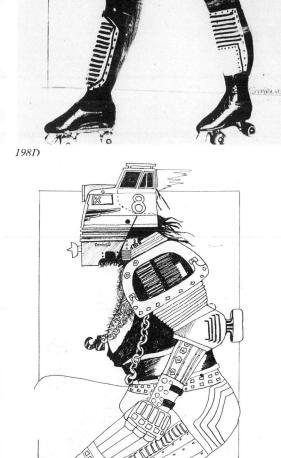

prophetic Sean Kenny, however, who enjoyed a teemingly successful collaboration with Lionel Bart, they have been starved of opportunity, unless they designed contemporary operas for companies such as the ENO and its Welsh and Scottish equivalents. But from the moment when Timothy O'Brien – an associate designer of the RSC – and his colleague Tazeena Firth were invited by Hal Prince to design *Evita*, things changed rapidly and irrevocably.

At that point there was a confluence between British popular entertainment and British classical theatre, a theatre which had developed with unprecedented rapidity under the patronage of state subsidy. In the subsidized theatres of the National and the RSC, designers had continuity of employ, the opportunity to make artistic marriages with directors and indeed writers, and the stimulus of an expanding repertoire of English and European classic plays in many styles and disciplines. Conversely, they also understood the need for unusual flexibility, control and technical efficiency required by the repertoire system, where huge productions had to be changed from one to another, frequently between matinee and evening performances.

Major theatre companies were congratulated during the 1970s for achieving a 'house style', which more often that not meant that they were presenting a synthesis of design ideas rather than a shared acting style. The raked stage offered up and focused plays of heightened language; real materials like wood and iron, sand and rope and the bricks of the building removed all sense of decoration, and design became a matter of space and extended metaphor. My colleague Christopher Morley once remarked, 'There are limitless opportunities for the destruction of scenery.' Designers began to consider with their directors not just the stage on which a production was to happen but the building, the environment,

198A–D **Starlight Express**. Music Andrew Lloyd Webber. Lyrics Richard Stilgoe

DESIGNER JOHN NAPIER: 'We had to find a practical and dynamic solution to a piece where all the actors were on skates all the time. So we had them moving on a continuing spiral which raked through the proscenium into, and right round, the auditorium; and they got from level to level on a bridge which interlocked. To do this we took out a thousand seats, but the theatre still held around 1,700 people.'

ASSOCIATE COSTUME DESIGNER LIZ DA COSTA: 'The costumes had to combine special safety requirements for roller skating with dance mobility and train characteristics. The main considerations were a lively appearance without attempting realism, and materials which would withstand the tough demands of the show.'

198C   Headdresses and make-up for the engines
198D   Costume design for British engine
198E   Working drawing for one of the Greaseball gang; ideas developed from this

Apollo Victoria, London, 1984
Director Trevor Nunn
Lighting David Hersey
Photograph by David Crosswaite (198A) of the model with John Napier behind
Photograph by David Crosswaite (198B) of the set being constructed

198D

198E

155

199A

199B

and every influence on the public from the moment of arrival. In a chicken-and-egg kinship, productions strove to become events to be 'experienced' rather than observed, and companies in their turn strove to choose plays that could legitimately expand into 'total-theatre happenings'. The coming together of classical and popular streams was probably inevitable, but when it happened the bigger budget expenditure possible on large-scale musicals liberated the daring and technological expertise of designers constrained by the rules of repertoire, and gave a potent stimulus to a huge and quite different audience. 'Scenery' disappeared and environments and machines took its place.

Timothy O'Brien, Ralph Koltai, Farrah, John Gunter, Bill Dudley, Maria Björnson and most influentially John Napier – who between them have designed most of the big British musicals of the decade – had all worked for both the National and the RSC, solving the brain-teasing problems of presenting a wide variety of classic and contemporary theatre in repertoire. They had frequently collaborated, recognizing the need to give and take. They became a collective influence on each other, as they proved their flexibility and their lack of inhibition whilst retaining highly recognizable artistic signatures.

Subsidized classical theatre has known many periods of belt-tightened austerity when the philosophy of bare empty spaces for the presentation of actors and language has sometimes become an excuse for absence of ideas. But equally some theatre journalists see a spectacular design solution as evidence that the production is without intellectual content, or that the text has not been rigorously investigated. 'I came out humming the sets' – a wickedly scathing Noël Coward *bon mot* – has become something of a critical *donnée*, warning us that designer domination is contagious, and that to feast the eyes destroys the other senses. Designers often encounter a low level of understanding and appreciation of their work. What they find most depressing of all is when tawdry revivals of 'classic' Fifties musicals arrive in the West End, as they do, with shabby replicas of original Fifties scenery, to be enthusiastically welcomed for their visual delights. I have heard countless designers declare, 'Why do we bother?' They find solace and

199C

199A–C **The Phantom of the Opera**. Music Andrew Lloyd Webber. Lyrics Charles Hart. Book Richard Stilgoe (also additional lyrics) and Andrew Lloyd Webber, based on Gaston Leroux's novel

DESIGNER MARIA BJÖRNSON: 'Against the backdrop of the Paris Opéra we used drapes swagging downwards and upwards, dark Turkish corners leading off to nowhere, and candles rising out of the floor through mist, as devices to underline the repressed Victorian sensuality and ritualistic quality of the piece.'

199B Storyboard: a work-out of early ideas

Her Majesty's Theatre, London, 1986
Director Harold Prince
Lighting Andrew Bridge
Production photographs by Clive Barda (199A&C)
Michael Crawford (The Phantom, *199A & C*), Sarah Brightman (Christine, *199A*)

157

200A

200B

200C

200D

confirmation in each other. Directors tend to stay remote from their colleagues; conductors are nakedly competitive; writers cultivate lacerating disdain of their rivals. Amongst designers there is, though, a noticeable camaraderie and a familial kinship. They know that just keeping the flame alight is difficult; to make it burn hard and gem-like is more difficult when very few will notice the difference.

In the ten years coming up designers will have to fight harder than ever before, not just for the recognition they deserve, but for their share of the resources with which to do things. Extravagance is a criticism always levelled against the theatre, subsidized or commercial, and extravagance invariably means the design budget.

The extraordinary achievements of the last decade in all forms of theatre in Britain, but especially in musical theatre, will only be equalled if there is the same vital combination of funds, trust and daring to support the frontier-expanding solutions, with which directors and designers challenge acceptance of what is possible and impossible. Risk produces the unexpected which, in every sense, keeps us alive.

The author is the director of Cats, Starlight Express, Chess, Aspects of Love, *and* Les Misérables *(this last with John Caird); also of many plays and operas. He was artistic director of the Royal Shakespeare Company from 1968 to 1978, and joint artistic director from 1978 to 1987.*

200A–D **Me and My Girl**. Book and lyrics L. Arthur Rose and Douglas Furber, revised Stephen Fry. Music Noel Gay

SET DESIGNER MARTIN JOHNS: 'Although the piece is set in the late Thirties, we wanted to avoid a Thirties staging where the major scene changes were hidden by a front cloth. Our priority was to make all twelve changes part of the action, and alter the locations in front of the audience.'

COSTUME DESIGNER ANN CURTIS: 'These are the Lambeth mates of Cockney Bill in the brash "Pearly" finery they wore to gatecrash the Duchess's formal cocktail party (*200D*), when two totally different societies clashed, to be eventually united by the free and easy charm of The Lambeth Walk.'

200A   The kitchen in Hareford House
200B   The house and garden
200C   A street corner in Lambeth

Haymarket Theatre, Leicester, 1984
Director Mike Ockrent
Lighting Chris Ellis
Set photographs by Laurence Southon

201A

201B

201A & B **Alice in Wonderland**. Lewis Carroll. Adaptation and lyrics John Wells. Music Carl Davis

DESIGNER ANTHONY WARD: 'The magic garden discovered by Alice through the door was a vastly magnified and grotesque version of a glass dome seen at the start of the production on a piano (*201A*). All her adventures were visually rooted in the reality of her Victorian childhood.'

201B Costume drawing for Bill Lizard

Lyric Theatre, Hammersmith, 1986
Director Ian Forrest
Lighting Richard Caswell
Production photograph by Donald Cooper (201A)
Lesley Manville (Alice)

202 **Kiss Me Kate**. Music Cole Porter. Book Sam and Bella Spewack

COSTUME DESIGNER LIZ DA COSTA: 'Though the musical is set in the Forties, the taming of the shrew play-within-the-play was given in Elizabethan clothes. For musical episodes we used eccentric fabrics and designs which allowed energetic dancing while keeping a period flavour.'

Royal Shakespeare Company, 1987
Director Adrian Noble
Set designer William Dudley
Lighting Mark Henderson
Production photograph by David Crosswaite
From left: Tricia Tomlinson (Babs), Cyril Nri (Chas Gilpin/Gremio), Peter Ledbury (Benjamin Stubbs/Hortensio), Marisa Campbell (Vera) Tim Flavin (Bill Calhoun/Lucentio)

202

161

203A–C **Time.** Book and lyrics David Soames. Music Jeff
Daniels. Book, music and lyrics co-written by Dave Clark

DESIGNER JOHN NAPIER: 'A musical that was as close as you
could get to a big rock-and-roll event; and because it was also
about space it gave me an unmissable chance to use modern
technology to the limit.'

The Dominion Theatre, London, 1986
Director Larry Fuller
Lighting Andrew Bridge
Production photographs by Nobby Clark
203A John North (Judge Trigon)
203B Melchisedec's retinue
203C David Cassidy (Chris Wilder), Maria Ventura, Stephanie
Lawrence, Dawn Hope (Carol-Ann, Louise, Babs), David Timpson, Jan
Servais, John North (Judges Lagos, Morgua, Trigon), Jeff Shankley
(Lord Melchisedec)

203A   *203C*

203B

204

204 **The Wizard of Oz**. L. Frank Baum. Music and lyrics of the MGM picture score, Harold Arlen and E. Y. Harburg. Book adapted by John Kane

DESIGNER MARK THOMPSON: 'We evolved a homage to the American movie, attempting to be truthful to the film yet quite different in concept. Here Munchkinland is revealed as a pastiche of early Hollywood.'

Royal Shakespeare Company, 1987
Director Ian Judge
Lighting Nick Chelton
Production photograph by Clive Barda
Imelda Staunton (Dorothy), Dilys Laye (Glinda)

205 **Are You Lonesome Tonight**? Alan Bleasdale

DESIGNER VOYTEK: 'A play with Elvis Presley songs became a musical on a monument representing his mis-spent life. The unveiling of a white satin shroud revealed a pile of records, guitars, film-cans, gold lamé and Cadillacs, with the band like a cherry on top of an ice-cream sundae.'

Phoenix Theatre, London, 1985
Director Robin Lefèvre
Lighting Dave Horn
Production photograph by Joe Roman
Simon Bowman (Young Presley)

205

164

206A

206B

206C

206A–E **Guys and Dolls**. Music and lyrics Frank Loesser. Book Jo Swerling and Abe Burrows (from Damon Runyon)

SET DESIGNER JOHN GUNTER: 'The design was conceived out of a great love for the American musical of the Fifties and Sixties. The idea was to have two New Yorks – by day, drab and seedy; by night, glitter, neon and exciting.'

206A   Night-time New York
206B   Day-time New York
206C   The sewer where the guys held their crap game

COSTUME DESIGNER SUE BLANE: 'In the "A Bushel and a Peck" number, with Miss Adelaide dressed in gingham carrying a pitchfork, it seemed right to dress the girls as chickens – Rhode Island Reds (*206D*). For the gangsters, to repeat the neon of the set, strong colours were used: classic pin stripes in orange or red, for instance, wide-brimmmed hats in pink and yellow, two-tone shoes in brown and lilac (*206E*).'

National Theatre (Olivier), 1982
Director Richard Eyre
Lighting David Hersey
Set photographs by Group Three Photography (206A–C)

HOT-BOX GIRLS
"BUSHEL AND A PECK"

HARRY THE HORSE

BIG JULE

BILL PATERSON

JIM CARTER

207 Ziegfeld.
Book Ned Sherrin and Alastair Beaton. Score devised by Michael Reed

DESIGNER ROBIN DON: 'To an orchestral crescendo from Puccini's *Madam Butterfly* the petals open revealing the awakening dragonfly. She spreads her wings and flies, creating a mirthful moment in this 37-scene extravaganza.'

London Palladium, 1988
Conceived, choreographed and directed by Joe Layton
Costume designer Theoni Aldredge
Lighting Tharon Musser
Production photograph by Richard McLaren
Jacey Collins (the Dragonfly)

206E

206D

207

208A

208B

208C

208A–C **Metropolis**. Based on Fritz Lang's film (1926). Book and lyrics Joe Brooks and Dusty Hughes. Music Joe Brooks

DESIGNER RALPH KOLTAI: 'A musical that depicts an élitist society whose frivolous lifestyle is maintained by subjugated and enslaved workers. The three-dimensional steel front "curtain" (208C), which divided into two horizontally, was intended to convey the hardness of the subject. The costume drawing (208B) is of Futura, a robot, who acquires a human quality. The production photograph (208A) shows the machine room; part of it revolved to reveal the furnace in which Futura was burned.'

Piccadilly Theatre, London, 1989
Director Jerome Savary
Lighting David Hersey
Photographs by Ralph Koltai

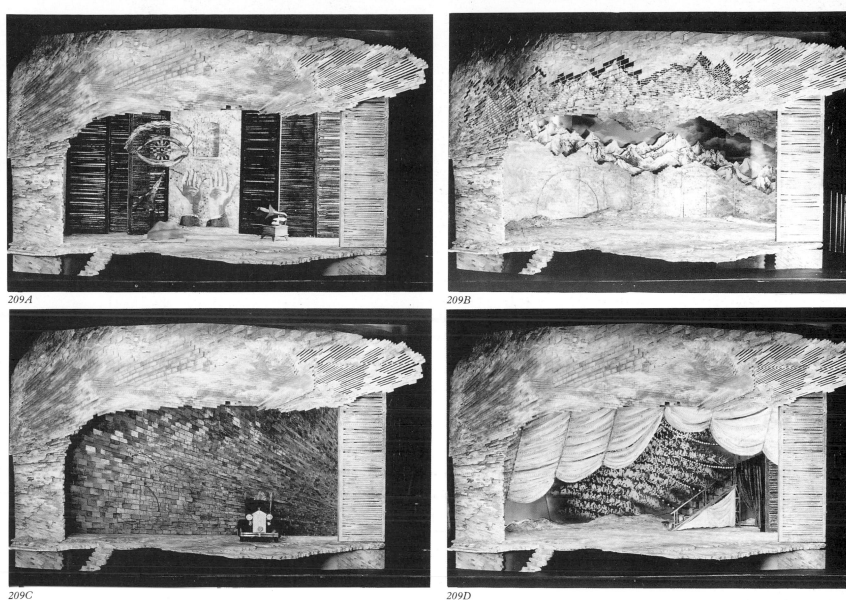

209A *209B* *209C* *209D*

209A–D **Aspects of Love**. Music Andrew Lloyd Webber. Lyrics Don Black and Charles Hart. Story from David Garnett's novel

DESIGNER MARIA BJÖRNSON: 'The sequence here is of the model, and shows some of the many scenes: the Surrealist exhibition in Paris (*209A*); the day-trip to the Pyrenees (*209B*); Rose's journey to Paris – back-projected on the gauze (*209C*); the circus – the cast sit in the stepped seats, right, and merge with pictured audience on backdrop (*209D*).'

Prince of Wales Theatre, London, 1989
Director Trevor Nunn
Lighting Andrew Bridge
Model photographs by David Crosswaite

DANCE

MARY CLARKE AND
CLEMENT CRISP

Anyone designing for dance has to be aware of the special rules and conditions that concern movement in a theatrical space. The first, and most obvious, is the fact of movement itself. Bodies in motion must be free from physical constraint, and dance dictates that the shape of the bodies, and the stretch of limbs and trunk, must be absolutely clear to the audience. Furthermore, the interrelationship between a setting and costumes becomes, in a dance performance, a matter of a sophisticated balance between the immobility of the setting and the mobility of the cast. Fluidity and physical freedom – so essential for the art – will present inevitable problems for the designer who must try to reflect the quicksilver of the language without losing sight of the sense and context of the work as a whole.

Designs for dance set mood, and establish a first basis for the audience's understanding of what is to happen. Decoration must, therefore, be exceptionally sensitive to the choreographer's intention: the language spoken by the decorator must be that of the dance creator. With no printed text or other record to fall back upon, a dance audience relies upon information – direct or allusive – given by the decorator about the work to be seen. In such traditional ballets as *The Sleeping Beauty* or *Romeo and Juliet*, the tasks are those of establishing location and providing suitable historical dress. But with a plotless ballet – the music serving as a foundation upon which the choreographer has created a structure of movement – the designer must provide sympathetic surroundings, which will illuminate the dance's intentions and perhaps even guide the audience's feelings in those first crucial moments after curtain up, when the public is looking for messages about what is to follow.

Such ideally responsive design is not common, but we would cite a wonderful accord in the sets and costumes designed by Sophie Fedorovitch for the plotless

210

210 **Pulcinella**. Richard Alston

DESIGNER HOWARD HODGKIN

Rambert Dance Company, 1987
Lighting Peter Mumford
Production photograph by Catherine Ashmore
Amanda Britton (Pimpinella), John Carney (Pulcinella), Sara Matthews, Alexandra Dyer, Lucy Bethune

171

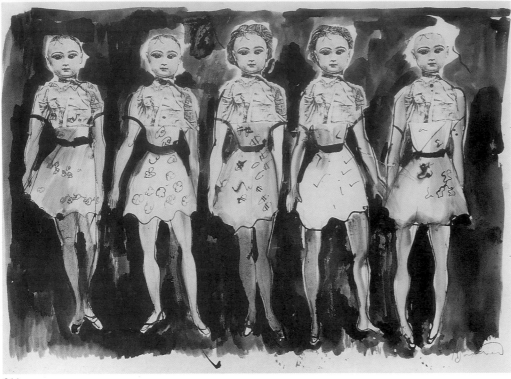

211

211 **My Brother, My Sisters**. Kenneth MacMillan

DESIGNER YOLANDA
SONNABEND

Stuttgart Ballet, 1978
Costume designs for the sisters
(Private collection)

sublimitics of Frederick Ashton's *Symphonic Variations* in 1946, and also the eminently responsive decoration made by Yolanda Sonnabend for Kenneth MacMillan's *My Brother, My Sisters*, where neurotic tensions between the members of a family were framed and coloured by a design evoking the brooding air of menace which was the matter of the ballet.

Design for dance is also, of course, dictated by its theatrical location. Once dance was only to be found in opera houses – its design thus affected by the established formulae of nineteenth-century decorative style – but it is now to be seen in any and every locale. The opera house and the traditional proscenium theatre still claim a lion's share of performance, and propose conventional decoration, but modern and post-modern dance have ventured into art galleries and public places, into streets and disused factory spaces. And these new homes have brought new challenges and new rewards for the designer. Meanwhile, the different audience that has emerged in Britain, as modern and post-modern dance have begun to seize the imagination of a predominantly young generation, has meant a fresh concept for dance clothes and settings. Paul Dart provided the costuming for *Rite Elektrik*, a creation for London Contemporary Dance Theatre by Tom Jobe, in which the cast were dressed in the latest fashions of bondage gear to be found in the clubs frequented by the young audience, seeing themselves on stage in only slightly exaggerated dress. And in the camp excesses of the outré fashion provided by the Australian designer Leigh Bowery, and Body Map, for Michael Clark's extravaganzas, a young public was stimulated by clothes which they admired – a heightened and anarchic form of the dress they chose to wear in daily life. Dance design can, and should, reflect advanced forms of popular taste.

Fashion should also speak, as it did in American Ballet Theatre's 1988 restaging of Massine's *Gaieté Parisienne* – costumed by Christian Lacroix, the newest hero of Parisian *haute couture*. But ballet has all too rarely called upon high fashion to dress dancers. Since Diaghilev's use of Chanel for *Le Train Bleu*, there have been few examples of ballets with couturier clothes, though Roland Petit used Dior and Yves St Laurent with notable success. It has been the Rambert Dance Company, under Richard Alston's directorate during recent years, which has shown the greatest awareness of the validity of fashion and fine art as companions to dancing: designers Katherine Hamnett, for Alston's *Strong Language*, and Victor Edelstein, for *Rhapsody in Blue*, have produced stylish costuming. Earlier Robert Cohan had invited Bill Gibb to design the clothes for his amusing *Waterless Method of Swimming Instruction*.

Alston's early training as an art student clearly predisposed him to inviting painters to design ballets for his company. In his earliest days he had staged dances in an art gallery where there was an exhibition of Jasper Johns's work. For his own creations in the Rambert repertoire he turned with success to painters and sculptors. Howard Hodgkin produced brilliantly coloured sets for *Pulcinella* and *Night Music*; Richard Smith decorated *Wildlife*; *Zansa* was designed by John Hoyland; and the sculptor Nigel Hall provided a structure for *Soda Lake*. Other works in the Rambert repertoire gained from the involvement of painters, Ashley Page's *Carmen Arcadiae* was dazzlingly designed by Jack Smith and – in an experimental evening of new choreography, given under the significant title of *Collaborations* – John Murphy, Richard

Deacon and Anish Kapoor were involved in the creation of workshop productions. This policy also brought a fascinating contribution by Stephen Buckley to the creation of a ballet by Mary Evelyn, *Trace*. One other earlier use of an easel painter was highly effective when, in 1983, Robert North, then director of the company, invited Bridget Riley to provide settings for his ballet *Colour Moves*. The subtle relationships between colours in Bridget Riley's designs – which happily adapted her easel style to the theatre – were the starting point for the danced text itself, and the ballet was a constant delight to the eye.

In the mid-Eighties the Royal Opera House, Covent Garden, also made a conscious attempt to expand its decorative range. The art critic Bryan Robertson was appointed as design consultant, his brief to suggest artists who had not previously designed for the stage. This was a reversion to an earlier and, alas, lost tradition. In the Thirties and Forties, Ninette de Valois's ballet had called upon such eminent figures as Edward Burra, Graham Sutherland, Rex Whistler, John Piper and Leslie Hurry, and had gained thereby magnificent decoration for the repertoire. Thus it was that Patrick Caulfield, Deanna Petherbridge, Christopher Lebrun, Victor Pasmore, Helen Frankenthaler, and John Hubbard were invited to design a series of new works. But with such powerful and mature painters, and with the implicit idea that the design was 'important', the young choreographers were not always able to maintain their own creative balance with the design. Michael Corder, a gifted young dance-maker, found his movement somehow oppressed by the emphatic imagery of Caulfield's Opera House fantasy in *Party Game*, and his subsequent collaboration with the American painter Helen Frankenthaler was far from happy. She overloaded his *Number Three* with three backdrops – two of them very fine, however – and provided costuming completely out of harmony with Corder's wishes. The ballet had to be performed alternately in the Frankenthaler-designed costumes, and in simple white leotards of the choreographer's choice, so that the public might see his dances more clearly on the 'white' nights. The John Hubbard designs for Richard Alston's *Midsummer* looked no more than

easel painting enlarged as a background for the dance; it was only Victor Pasmore's austere and evocative settings that worked in aesthetic harmony with David Bintley's Attic simplicity for *Young Apollo*.

An appalling fruit of this policy, and one of the worst stagings ever perpetrated by the Royal Ballet, was Christopher Lebrun's decoration for the revival of *Ballet Imperial* in 1985. This Balanchine masterpiece already had a bizarre design history at the Opera House. Originally presented at Covent Garden in 1950, it had been given sets and costumes of superb quality by Eugène Berman. Because Balanchine sought later to get away from the 'imperial' connotations of the piece – even re-naming it *Piano Concerto Number Two* – it was, at the choreographer's request, given less specific decoration by Carl Toms, and was then further redecorated by Terence Emery, neither revision obliterating memories of Berman's decor, which was an outstanding example of this great stage designer's style. Lebrun's lumpen decorations for the 1985 revival (plus anonymous and vulgar costuming) were entirely unsuited to the style of the ballet, though they were, alas, apt in reflecting both the dismal technical performances of the cast, and the brutish revival of the choreography itself.

Among the most impressive painterly designs at the Opera House, or elsewhere, in recent years has been Jack Smith's 1987 decoration for Ashley Page's *Pursuit* for the Royal Ballet. Page's hard-edged and energetic classic steps were well matched by the uncompromising colours of Smith's set and the sharp outlines of the dancers' costumes (reminiscent of Schlemmer's tutus in *The Triadic Ballet* at the Bauhaus). Here painter and choreographer were speaking the same language. In one other work, Frederick Ashton's *Varii Capricii*, dance and design were happily at one; created for Sibley and Dowell, the ballet was an amused comment on human foibles, and David Hockney provided sunny and lighthearted decoration to set the mood for this sophisticated frolic.

In the more conventional relationship between choreographer and professional designer, the last decade has seen the emergence of gifted stage decorators, as well as some impressive and long-standing collaborations. The partnership between Nicholas Georgiadis and Kenneth MacMillan is an example of two creators working with a clear common purpose. This has found an interesting parallel in the stagings by David Bintley with the designer Terry Bartlett. Their first joint venture was Bintley's full-length *Swan of Tuonela* for Sadler's Wells Royal Ballet in 1982. Bintley's bardic recreation of Finnish legend found an exact visual response in Bartlett's designs. Bartlett was subsequently to decorate several more works for Bintley, in each case finding a clear image that seemed to spring from the dance itself. He also produced an outstanding permanent set for Peter Darrell's full-length *Carmen* for the Scottish Ballet: a double-tiered curve of arches backed by wooden shutters, into which various properties were dropped to suggest different locations.

The decade also saw an exceptional contribution to the dance stage by Yolanda Sonnabend, both a painter and stage-designer. In addition to *Swan Lake*, for Anthony Dowell at the Royal Opera House, which we discuss elsewhere, she developed a relationship with the work of Kenneth MacMillan, producing design of rare emotional resonance and variety of style. She had earlier decorated three MacMillan ballets, including the Japanese study *Rituals* and the contemplative *Requiem* – first given in Stuttgart in 1976 and revived at Covent Garden in 1983. With *My Brother, My Sisters*, she shaped a richly allusive setting to focus on the brooding emotions of an extraordinary family. With *Playground*, for the Sadler's Wells Royal Ballet, she made a completely realistic wired enclosure in which a group of mad people played out their personal dramas like schoolchildren. In *Valley of Shadows* she produced a view of an Italian garden replete with symbols of mortality as a premonition of the terrors, the ashen clothing and bleak walls of a death camp. One other work designed by Yolanda Sonnabend during this period must be mentioned: her poetic response to the world of the Duparc songs that were the text for Michael Corder's *L'Invitation au voyage*. The cast seemed like revenants returned to the skeletal golden pavilion that was part of Sonnabend's nacreous and exquisite setting.

Of the various other works which have entered the Royal Ballet repertoire during this period, some are most kindly passed over in silence. We must, though, salute the simplicity and emotional force of Andy Klunder's stark set for MacMillan's *Gloria*, in which the ghosts of men killed in the trenches of the First World War returned to their womenfolk; and two bold designs by Georgiadis for one-act ballets – MacMillan's *Orpheus* and Rudolf Nureyev's *The Tempest*.

Another who has proved equally felicitous with short ballets as with larger works is the producer–designer Philip Prowse. For the joint Festival Ballet–ENO Bartok celebration in 1981 he, with Geoffrey Cauley as choreographer, produced a boldly imagined version of *The Wooden Prince* in terms of the Chinese theatre. For Michael Corder's *Gloriana* for Sadler's Wells Royal Ballet in 1987 Prowse contrived a visual essence of the Elizabethan age haunted by an awareness of death; black-garbed courtiers were seen against architectural elements taken from interiors of the period.

The collaboration between a designer and a choreographer may extend over a period of several years and many works. David Bintley's earliest ballets in the last ten years found lively response in the decoration provided by Mike Beckett. Nadine Baylis's long-term relationship with the choreographies of Glen Tetley was especially noteworthy in their full-length *The Tempest* staged by Ballet Rambert in 1979. The design showed a fantastic world of billowing fabric, the setting offering cloth sails transformed by projections, and with an immense nylon sheet to suggest the sea. Producing a rather different fantasy for London Contemporary Dance Theatre in *Phantasmagoria* in 1987, Nadine Baylis was required to provide a series of sleight-of-hand tricks as part of the production's magic lantern imagery.

In its first seasons during the late Sixties and early Seventies, London Contemporary Dance could afford only to offer basic design. There soon emerged – thanks to the involvement of the designers Norberto Chiesa and Peter Farmer – a more positive visual impact for the repertoire, an impact typified by Robert Cohan's *Stages*, with its hallucinatory Farmer designs. The repertoire was also much enhanced by

212 **Rushes**.
Siobhan Davies

DESIGNER DAVID
BUCKLAND

Rambert Dance Company, 1987
Lighting Peter Mumford
Production photograph by David Buckland
From left: Michael Hodges,
Siobhan Stanley, Ben Craft

212

the excellence of the lighting. It must be said that to this day it is LCDT which best understands the potential of light to create atmosphere and to illuminate, in the truest sense, the art of the dancer. In more recent years the collaboration between the choreographer Siobhan Davies and the photographer –designer David Buckland has provided an intriguing new aspect to the decoration of dance, photographic images, in a work like *Rushes*, seeming an extension and an echo of the dance itself.

The generation of dance creators which emerged in the wake of LCDT – to produce the 'New Dance' of today – offer a rather more mundane view of design. Though costuming is functional, tediously related to street dress, nevertheless designers are often closely involved with the creation of this post-modern repertoire, as can be seen in the work of Antony McDonald for Second Stride. Rosemary Butcher, too, is noteworthy. She produces dances in which movement is contained within a severely limited range, and she has chosen to work in close collaboration with the sculptor Heinz-Dieter Pietsch.

For the majority of the ballet public, seeing dance means going to watch the full-length works, both classical and modern, which remain the big box-office draw in almost every dance centre. It is the Royal Ballet which has, during the past fifty years, shown the continuing vitality of the nineteenth-century classics for a devoted audience. The company has also demonstrated that this repertoire of full-length pieces may be augmented by contemporary choreographers: the pioneering creations of Sir Frederick Ashton – *Cinderella*, *La Fille mal Gardée* and *Ondine* – were to be added to by a second generation of British choreographers, John Cranko and Kenneth MacMillan, who produced full-length ballets of huge popularity.

The tradition thus established in the Royal Ballet meant that major works had then to be produced to develop the repertoire and to provide new opportunities for dancers and choreographers. The last decade began well with the resounding success of Kenneth MacMillan's *Mayerling*. MacMillan's purpose was to show the haunted and tragic figure of the Archduke Rudolf in the historical and emotional circumstances

213

214

which occasioned his death. For Nicholas Georgiadis – MacMillan's favoured designer since his very first ballets in the Fifties – the task was to recreate the world of Hapsburg Vienna at its very stuffiest. The action had to move between the claustrophobic grandeur of the Hofburg and a louche tavern; between a scene in the wintry countryside featuring a hunting party and the drawing room of the Vetsera household; between the hunting lodge at Mayerling and the graveyard where Mary Vetsera was secretly interred. Georgiadis achieved all this through constructed sets which proved easy to change yet were convincingly real, and through painted drops. The fluidity of the stage design was matched by the mobility of costume – so essential for dancers. In a ballet where historical verisimilitude was necessary in order to establish the 'look' of the period – conveying the social exterior of Rudolf's inner despairs – Georgiadis had to find a way of showing the elaboration of court uniform and the heavy outline of women's dress in the age of the bustle, whilst freeing bodies to encompass the full range of the choreography, which sometimes needed to be expressively violent. Georgiadis contrived to capture the essence of shapes and of the formal magnificence of clothing through materials that were light in movement but rich in decoration and always maintaining a proper air of opulence. The colour tones were often dark, richly glowing. The result suggested period authenticity without constraining the poetic liberties and allusions

213 **Orpheus**. Kenneth MacMillan

DESIGNER NICHOLAS GEORGIADIS

Royal Ballet, 1982
Lighting John B. Read
Production photograph by Leslie E. Spatt

214 **Mayerling**. Kenneth MacMillan

DESIGNER NICHOLAS GEORGIADIS

Royal Ballet, 1978
Lighting David Hersey
Model photograph of Act 1, Scene 2 by Donald Southern

which are essential to ballet, and without at any moment constraining the dancers' bodies. *Mayerling*, like the earlier MacMillan–Georgiadis collaborations of *Romeo and Juliet* and *Manon*, represents an apogee of grand opera-house design. Not literal, nor fantasticated, it shows design entirely in harmony with choreographic approach and theme.

In 1981 MacMillan was to produce another full-length work on an historical character. His *Isadora* was an attempt further to break the conventions of evening-long balletic narrative. It involved a double portrayal of Duncan – by the ballerina Merle Park and the actress Mary Miller, who spoke Isadora's words. MacMillan sought to surmount what he saw as the barriers between the ballet and the theatre by a production which was adventurous in form and content, and he turned to Barry Kay, who had in 1971 provided outstanding designs for his *Anastasia*. For the constantly shifting locations and timescale of *Isadora* Kay chose a curtain on a semi-circular track, which enabled swift, cinematic dissolves of scene; his clothing made vividly theatrical the everyday dress worn throughout the ballet's timescale of three decades.

MacMillan's big ballets are that necessary extension for today's public of the traditional 'classics' of the nineteenth century. The ubiquitous *Swan Lake* alone has received four very different treatments. For the Royal Ballet at Covent Garden in 1987 Yolanda Sonnabend produced opulent decoration which seemed characteristic of the company's elaborate conception of the way the classics should be presented. The present needs of companies to take a fresh look at a staple of the repertoire was also evident in London Festival Ballet's acquisition of Natalia Makarova's radical *Swan Lake*, in which a condensed text was seen as a paradigm of classical dancing, and placed by the German designer Gunther Schneider-Siemsson in an allusive set of wing shapes, on which were projected scenic decoration. A more traditional approach was adopted by Tim Goodchild for a joint Anglo-Soviet production mounted for the Moscow Classical Ballet on a British tour during the summer of 1988. We record, however, that it was Philip Prowse who created the most visually stimulating presentation of *Swan Lake* – in his version designed for Sadler's Wells Royal Ballet in 1981. Peter Wright's staging made innovations which did not disrupt the traditional values of the piece; Prowse's sets and costumes – wholly effective for a medium-sized touring company – were conceived in black shot with both gold and undercurrents of colour. The effect was of brooding mystery as well as of formal dignity, and the ballet appeared at its grandest. Prowse was also to be responsible for a no-less-successful *Sleeping Beauty* for Sadler's Wells Royal Ballet, in which an acute sense of period style, in decoration and in outline of dress, resulted in an evocation of French court life which is the basic matter of the ballet's architecture.

In the more elaborate context of an opera house production, David Walker made some revisions to his 1977 designs for *The Sleeping Beauty*, as presented by the Royal Ballet at Covent Garden, when he provided a new set for the Awakening scene. Walker has been most successful, though, in adapting Victorian decorative convention to the ballet stage: his 1979 designs for Bournonville's *La Sylphide* for London Festival Ballet was a skilled essay in domestic charm and the Highland scenery of the Romantic age.

Julia Trevelyan Oman, also an acute period stylist in decoration, had provided the sets and costumes for a new Royal Ballet production of *The Nutcracker* in 1984. The staging by Peter Wright restored the original Ivanov choreographic text and, by locating

215

215 **Giselle**. Marius Petipa after Jean Coralli and Jules Perrot

DESIGNER JOHN MACFARLANE

Royal Ballet, 1985
Director Peter Wright
Lighting Jennifer Tipton
Set photograph of Act 2 by Group Three Photography

the action very specifically in the Biedermeier tradition, Julia Trevelyan Oman produced a bewitching first act of German family life. Her second act was set in a Kingdom of Sweets inspired by the creamy delights of a cake which had featured in the first act.

The other two staples of the Royal Ballet's repertoire are *Giselle* and *Coppelia*. The first was unhappily redesigned by the late James Bailey in 1980 and then, five years later, given fresh decoration by John Macfarlane. Macfarlane seemed strongly influenced by the fact that Giselle's home is traditionally thought to be on the edge of a forest and that her burial place in Act II is located by a forest lake; he set Act I in a heavily wooded clearing and, to capture the haunted mystery of the second act, he made strong dramatic effect with the image of fallen trees arching over the stage action. *Coppelia* was freshly designed by Peter Snow for Sadler's Wells Royal Ballet in 1979, in an open-hearted version which stressed the peasant vitality of Hungarian folk dance.

Fashions change and dance changes too. The visual taste of an age changes as quickly. The enduring fact of dance is the movement itself. How it is dressed and the setting in which it finds itself is mutable. What endures in terms of design is for history to decide.

The co-authors of many books on dance, including Design for Ballet, *Mary Clarke is dance critic of the* Guardian *(since 1977) and editor of* Dancing Times *(since 1963), and Clement Crisp has contributed dance criticism to the* Financial Times *for thirty years.*

216

216 Rhapsody in Blue. Richard Alston

DESIGNER VICTOR EDELSTEIN: 'The dresses, Thirties-inspired, in different shades of blue chiffon with gold baroque embroideries, are intended to look extremely elegant and glamorous yet meet the rigorous demands of the dancers' movements.'

Rambert Dance Company, 1988
Lighting John B. Read
Production photograph by Catherine Ashmore
Alexandra Dyer, Siobhan Stanley, Sara Matthews

217 Zansa. Richard Alston

DESIGNER JOHN HOYLAND: 'I wanted the dance to take place within a changing dramatic setting. Having just finished a series of etchings each printed on three plates, I decided to adopt a similar method using three curtains. Each was an independent image, but they combined into a whole by the use of lighting and transparency.'

Rambert Dance Company, 1986
Lighting Peter Mumford
Production photograph by Catherine Ashmore
Foreground, from left: Cathrine Price, Robert Poole, Mary Evelyn, Mark Baldwin

218 Replacing. Lucy Bethune

SET DESIGNER RICHARD DEACON: 'The three parts of the set started stacked at the back of the stage, two of them concealing the third. Through the ballet the dancers turned the three parts. Each move exposed a previously hidden surface and left the set occupying more of the stage space.'

Rambert Dance Company, 1987
Costume designer Jacqueline Poncelet
Lighting Sid Ellen
Production photograph by Richard Deacon
From left: Glenn Wilkinson, Paul Old, Elizabeth Old, Michael Hodges, Rachel Lynch John

219 Colour Moves. Robert North

SET DESIGNER BRIDGET RILEY: 'There were five backcloths, four dominated by a single colour, the last (picture) all colours together. An abstract narrative emerged of contrast, harmony and warm and cold sensations which became the ballet's theme.'

Rambert Dance Company, 1983
Costume designer Andrew Storer
Lighting John B. Read
Production photograph by Anthony Crickmay
Dancer, Mary Evelyn

217

218

178

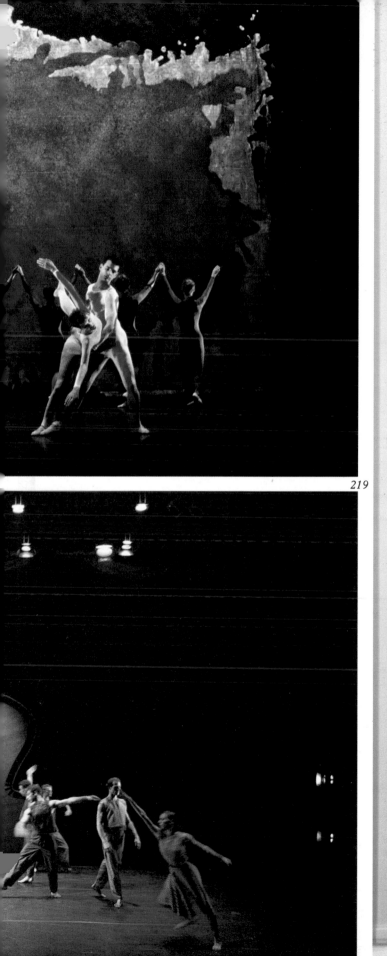

219

220A&B Chicanery.
Matthew Hawkins

DESIGNER PEARL (MARK ERSKINE-PULLIN): 'The piece was inspired by visits to Chiswick House. For the choreographer this became an essay on classical perspective and, for myself, on the similarities between 18th-century architecture and foundation garments – corsets, panniers and hiprolls. Each dancer had their own look. No colours were used, only black and white.'

Mantis Dance Company, 1984
Lighting Tim Barwick

221 Swan Lake.
Marius Petipa and Lev Ivanov

DESIGNER YOLANDA SONNABEND: 'This is the moment in the third act when von Rothbart and his familiars are introduced to the Princess with her ladies-in-waiting. The intention was to give the ballroom a glittering, jewelled, Fabergé quality which the costumes reflect.'

Royal Ballet, 1987
Director Anthony Dowell
Lighting John B. Read
Production photograph by Leslie E. Spatt
Derek Rencher (von Rothbart), Deanne Bergsma (the Princess)

222 La Sylphide.
Peter Schaufuss after August Bournonville

DESIGNER DAVID WALKER: 'Working within 19th-century conventions, an attempt was made to create a plausible reality for the ballet's Scottish background. The supernatural scenes thereby gained credibility in contrast with the (supposedly) real world.'

Costume design for the Sylph

London Festival Ballet, 1979
Lighting John B. Read

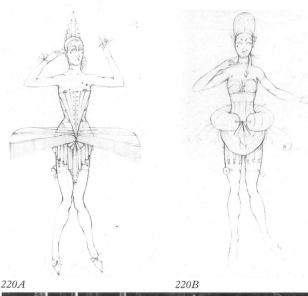

220A

220B

222

221

223 **Some Dance and
Some Duet**. Micha Bergese

DESIGNER LIZ DA COSTA:
'The addition of fringe on to
the basic leotard extended the
flow and motion of the dancers
to create new patterns of
movement.'

London Contemporary Dance
Theatre, 1980
Lighting Adrian Dightam
*Production photograph by
Anthony Crickmay*
Celia Hutton, Michael Small

223

224A

224A&B **The Sleeping Beauty**. Kenneth MacMillan after Marius Petipa

DESIGNER NICHOLAS GEORGIADIS: 'The main visual motif for this production is the wind-blown drapes of the Bavarian and Austrian Baroque. It seemed practical for a show that was intended for heavy touring and could not cope with a lot of architectural units.'

224A   The Hunt
224B   The Awakening

American Ballet Theatre, 1987
Lighting Thomas Skelton
Model photographs by Iris Argyropoulos

224B

225 **The Edge**.
Sian Williams

SET DESIGNER JENNIFER CAREY: 'This dance/play which takes place on a clifftop shows the relationship between a jealous, possessive mother and her rebellious daughter. The movement of the balloons filled with helium created a fragile elemental quality.'

The Kosh, 1987
Director Michael Merwitser
Costume designer Yvonne Deacon
Lighting Richard Johnston
Production photograph by Vicki Hallam
Sian Williams (the Daughter)

225

226 **A Simple Man**.
Gillian Lynne

DESIGNER TIM GOODCHILD: 'Lowry's paintings imposed a great discipline in colour and style. Every costume was first dyed and sprayed, then hand painted, every brush stroke from his work. Many hours were spent getting dancers to move with "big feet".'

Northern Ballet Theatre, 1987
Lighting Brian Harris
Production photograph by Linda Rich

227 **The Tempest**.
Glen Tetley

DESIGNER NADINE BAYLIS: 'The sea of silk, 16 yards square, became an integral part of the ballet.'

Rambert Dance Company, 1979
Lighting John B. Read
Production photograph courtesy the Norwegian Ballet whose revival is pictured here

227

229

228

228 Still Life at the Penguin Café. David Bintley

DESIGNER HAYDEN GRIFFIN: 'The ballet was conceived around extinct animals (or species threatened with extinction). The zebra's dance was one of six or seven dances by other animals from penguins to a human family; in the last number they all ended up in an ark.'

Costume design for the Cape Zebra

Royal Ballet, 1988
Lighting John B. Read

230

229 Trail. Gaby Agis

DESIGNER KATE BLACKER: 'Prefabricated corrugated iron curtain/floor structures imitated the backdrop/stage of conventional theatre, and provided a temporary site for each dancer within an art gallery, the Whitechapel, designed not for performance but for exhibitions. The audience, installation and dancers interacted and filled the entire gallery.'

Whitechapel Art Gallery, London, 1986
Lighting Kate Blacker
Production photograph by Kate Blacker
Dancer, Charlotte Zerbey

230 Rite Electrick. Tom Jobe

COSTUME DESIGNER PAUL DART: 'The costumes were based on leather and rubber "S & M" body harnesses. The sheer problem of getting such clothing to stay on, and be possible to dance in, shaped the final designs. Each costume was literally made on the dancer.'

London Contemporary Dance Theatre, 1984
Set and lighting Peter Mumford
Production photograph by Anthony Crickmay
Lauren Potter, Brenda Edwards

231

231 I am Curious Orange. Michael Clark

SET DESIGNER MICHAEL CLARK: 'This scene, with the Houses of Parliament in the background and the giant hamburger, is to do with the way American culture has swamped the world. It is a comment on the Americanization of Britain.'

Michael Clark and Company, 1988
Costume designers Body Map and Leigh Bowery
Lighting Charles Atlas
Production photograph by Richard Haughton
Brix Smith (on hamburger)

232 Berlin Requiem. Christopher Bruce

DESIGNER PAMELA MARRE: 'My brief was to produce a set that could change to serve two contrasting pieces – *Mahagonny* and *Das Berliner Requiem*. Networks of neon lights carried the message of consumer societies for the first; and when the lights of Mahagonny disappeared, a ruined structure was left for the bleak and prophetic Requiem.'

Part 1 of *Mahagonny* as filmed for television

Rambert Dance Company, 1982
Lighting Nick Chelton
Production photograph by Pamela Marre
From left: Cathrine Price, Lucy Burge, Lucy Bethune, Michael Ho, Diane Walker, Hugh Craig, Michael Popper

232

233 Soda Lake. Richard Alston

DESIGNER NIGEL HALL: '*Soda Lake* – named after an isolated dry lake in the Californian Mojave Desert – is a sculpture I made while living in Los Angeles in 1968. Intense emptiness, vast distance and silence are the dominant features of that landscape. Richard Alston saw the sculpture at a London exhibition of my work in 1980 and created the dance around it.'

Rambert Dance Company, 1986
Lighting Sid Ellen
Production photograph by Catherine Ashmore
Dancer, Mark Baldwin

233

235 Touch the Earth. Rosemary Butcher

SET DESIGNER HEINZ-DIETER PIETSCH: 'The installation is based on the ideas of land, territory, and its dispossessed, threatened peoples. An earth circle links basic, elementary sculptures: "screens" and "shields" to give shelter and protection, "poles", "spears" and "tools" to stake out land, to build on it, to defend and to work it.'

Rosemary Butcher Dance Company, 1987
Costume designer Gilly Dean
Lighting David Richardson
Production photography by Chris Ha
Dancer, Caroline Pegg

235

234 Fanfare für Tanzer. Ronald Hynd

DESIGNER PETER DOCHERTY; 'This plotless, all-male ballet could be interpreted as a fanfare for gymnasts or as a celebration of the 40th anniversary of peace after the Second World War. Its images are drawn from the steam-room, sauna, disco, gas-chamber.'

Bayerische Staatsoper, Munich, 1985
Lighting Peter Docherty
Production photograph Foto Studio Sabine Toepffer

234

236A–C Dancing to Paint. Micha Bergese

DESIGNER RALPH STEADMAN: 'On stage were three dancers and the superb guitarist and composer of the music, Juan Martin. The design was based on *347 Suite*, the astonishing graphic works – about youth and age – made by Picasso when he was 87. The backdrop could be changed merely by lighting it from different angles. Paintings in the spirit of Picasso were projected on to it and the floor.'

Queen Elizabeth Hall, 1988
Lighting Benny Ball
Model photographs by Ralph Steadman

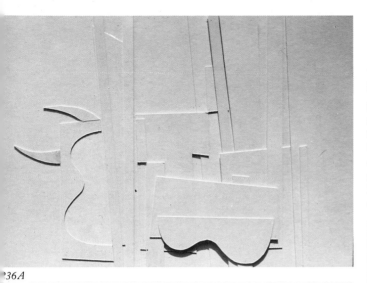

236A

236B

236C

237A&B **Crashed Car**. David Glass, text David Gale

DESIGNER RALPH STEADMAN: 'Part mime, part monologue, David Glass gave in this piece a solo performance as a psychiatrist who speaks with self-recrimination of his brother's death in an accident, and dramatically recreates it. Whereupon the wrecked car – whose base, hinged to the stage, had till then provided a backdrop (*237A*) – crashes violently forward, upright (*237B*).'

Tour, 1985
Director Hilary Westlake
Lighting Julian Sleath
Model photographs by Ralph Steadman

237A

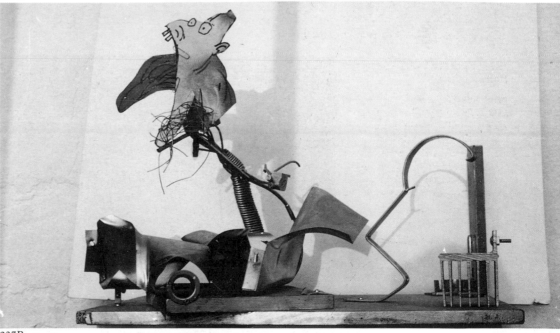

237B

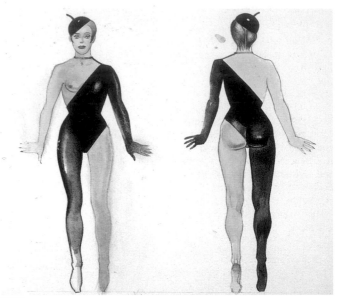

238A

238B

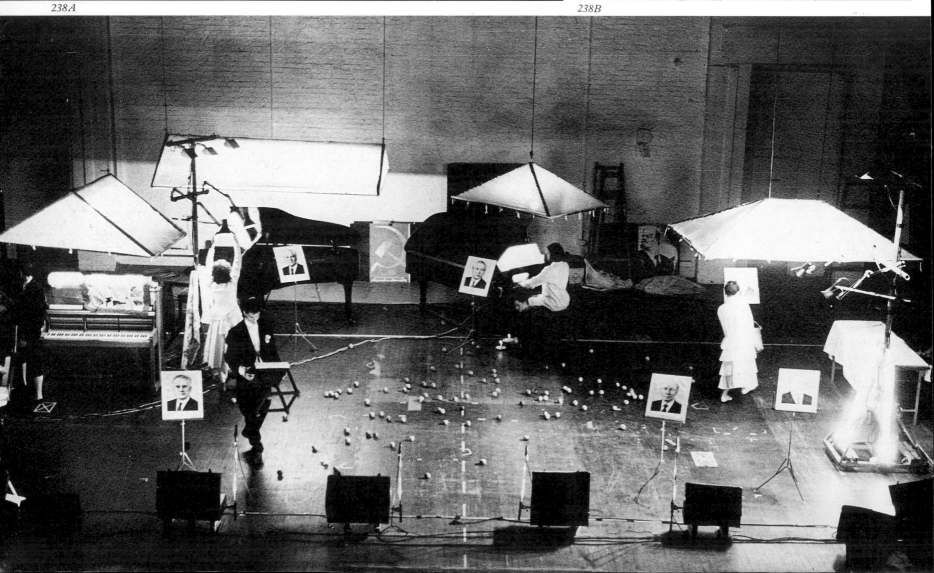

238A&B **Cinema**.
Richard Alston

DESIGNER ALLEN JONES:
'Upstage of the giant piano is a
floodlight illuminating the
notes; these provided an
entrance (*238A*).'

'In a 3-D form a contour
between two colours is often
more noticeable than the
contour of the form on which
it is painted. When the form is
self-evident, in this case the
bodies of the dancers (*238B*),
then colour can be used to
concentrate on the emotion of
the piece.'

Rambert Dance Company, 1989
Lighting Peter Mumford
Model photograph by Mike Owen

239 **Bösendorfer Waltzes**.
Ian Spink

DESIGNER ANTONY
McDONALD: 'This was an
attempt to break out of the
clinical look of many
contemporary dance pieces.
We did not use a dance lino
but the bare boards of
wherever we performed.
Objects, props, musical
instruments, musicians and
stage management were all
used to keep changing the
space and create
choreographic obstacles.'

Second Stride, 1986
Lighting Peter Mumford
Production photograph by Chris Ha

240 **Soldat**. Ashley Page

DESIGNER BRUCE McLEAN:
'I wanted the piece – a
contemporary version of
Stravinsky's *The Soldier's
Tale* (1918) – to look
applicable for 1989.'

Rambert Dance Company, 1988
Lighting Peter Mumford
*Production photograph by
Catherine Ashmore*
Mark Baldwin, Amanda Britton,
Paul Old, Gary Lambert

241 **Pribaoutki**.
Robert North

DESIGNER ANDREW
STORER: 'This ballet was
created as a homage to Picasso
on the centenary of his birth.
Each sequence was inspired by
a particular period of the
artist's work, or by individual
paintings as in the case of this
entr'acte which was developed
from the *Three Musicians*
painting of 1921.'

Rambert Dance Company, 1982
Lighting John B. Read
*Production photograph by
Catherine Ashmore*
Mary Evelyn, Michael Ho,
Michael Popper as the Three
Musicians

241

240

242 The Snow Queen.
David Bintley

DESIGNER TERRY
BARTLETT: 'David wanted
an environment in which
characters wove in and out en
route to the Snow Queen's
palace. The banners could be
flown out, but at the end, they
melt. I was inspired by the
stark church interiors in 17th-
century Dutch paintings, and
the organic forms of ice.

Sadler's Wells Royal Ballet, 1986
Lighting John B. Read
*Production photograph by
Leslie E. Spatt*
Samira Saidi (the Snow Queen)

243 The Swan of Tuonela.
David Bintley

DESIGNER TERRY
BARTLETT: 'The swan
cloak is the first image seen in
the ballet. Symbolic of good, it
is torn off by the demon Tuoni
and replaced at the end when
peace is restored. I wanted to
capture the spirit of a swan,
the idea of feathers and the
movement of wings, without
reverting to traditional
materials or the tutu.'

Sadler's Wells Royal Ballet, 1982
Lighting Mark Henderson
*Production photograph by
Leslie E. Spatt*
Dancer, June Highwood

242

243

244A–C Scared Shirtless.
Yolande Snaith

DESIGNER YOLANDE
SNAITH: 'Although not a
literal interpretation, the
dance was inspired by Gabriel
Garcia Marquez' book *One
Hundred Years of Solitude* –
images of love tragedies, of
bereft and solitary women.'

Institute of Contemporary Arts,
1987
Lighting Mike Seignior
*Production photographs by
Chris Nash*
Yolande Snaith

245 Dead Flight. Ian Spink

DESIGNER CRAIG GIVENS:
'The set, an eight by twelve
foot cutaway section of a
passenger airplane *c*.1940,
presented the isolation of
those in close proximity, and
the uncomfortable suspension
of time and place, contrasted
with the frenetic attempts of
people to engage with each
other in a crisis or disaster.'

Ian Spink Group, 1980
*Production photograph by
Dee Conway*
From left: Ian Spink, Betsy
Gregory, Beverly Sandwith,
Michele Smith, Eleanor Brickhill

244A

244B

244C

191

THE PAINTER AS DESIGNER

BRYAN ROBERTSON

David Hockney's courage and unselfconscious wit in designing so cheerfully for the stage from the mid-Sixties onwards created a more receptive climate for other artists inexperienced in stage design. Before then the practice of occasionally using painters to work in the theatre was beginning to recede, with the strong exceptions of Sidney Nolan's designs for Kenneth Macmillan's *Le Sacre du Printemps* in 1962, and Arthur Boyd's designs for Robert Helpmann's *Electra* in 1963. The unevenly successful but sometimes stirring stage work of John Piper, Graham Sutherland, Edward Burra, Osbert Lancaster, Kenneth Rowell, Isobel Lambert, Michael Ayrton, Robert Colquhoun and Robert MacBryde in the late Thirties and Forties – and Craxton, Hepworth and Noguchi in the Fifties – was becoming remote.

In the Fifties, for his one-act ballet, *La Péri* – to the great score by Dukas – Frederick Ashton used a sumptuous and characteristically long, horizontal picture by the celebrated landscape painter, Ivon Hitchens, to convey a generalized impression of a forest. To avoid issuing a commission for specific fresh designs, Ashton simply selected a work in Hitchens's studio to be enlarged in the Royal Ballet workshops – a dangerous procedure but doubtless the only solution to dealing with a comparatively unworldly painter who rarely left his Sussex studio set in dense plantations near Petworth.

Ashton's sense of Hitchens's suitability for this particular work was instinctive, however, in another critical dimension; he recognized the painter's innate sense of monumentality. The forms have a largeness which does not look merely inflated but appears to have a natural and inevitable scale of its own. Only rarely can painters or sculptors deal convincingly with the issue of large scale: often very big works are intrinsically small-scale in form as well as in content.

After a decade of severely elegant but almost empty stages for modern ballet – and some other theatre productions – which stylistically paralleled the bare minimalist abstraction in painting and sculpture from the mid-Sixties onwards, there was a real hunger for more visual excitement than that provided by a mobile unadorned lighting rig. The traditional idea of a painted backdrop providing colour and content, whether abstract or figurative, began to exert its appeal again. In 1973, Piper's Turneresque designs for Colin Graham's production of Britten's *Death in Venice* at the Royal Opera House had made a great impact, but Piper by then was a seasoned professional designer as well as a painter.

Enter Hockney. By 1978, when he was commissioned by John Cox to design *The Magic Flute* for Glyndebourne, he had already created *Ubu Roi* for the Royal Court Theatre in 1967 and the brilliantly successful *Rake's Progress*, also for Glyndebourne, in 1975. But although *The Magic Flute* was impressive, it seemed in essence to approximate more to a somewhat dehydrated and knowingly learned spectacle conceived within the dimensions of a toy theatre than to anything demanded by the work's grander or more fulsome scenes. Hockney's play with perspective and concern for the interplay between illusion and reality, constant through all his work in either painting or sculpture, here seemed intrusive.

Then in 1981 – as I have written elsewhere – came three works for the Metropolitan Opera in New York: Massine's ballet, *Parade*, for which Hockney had to

246A

246B

246A & B Backdrops for **Pursuit**, designed by JACK SMITH (Royal Ballet, 1987)

outstare the illustrious ghosts of Cocteau, Satie and Picasso; Poulenc's one-act opera derived from Apollinaire's poem, *Les Mamelles de Tirésias*, in which Hockney's love for Dufy first surfaced in his designs; and Ravel's one-act masterpiece of 1925, *L'Enfant et les Sortilèges*, composed to a libretto that Colette had written originally as a *ballet pour ma fille* – with Ravel firmly in mind – just before the First World War. (Ravel had the text with him when he was on active service as an ambulance driver.) John Dexter put these three works together – the linking themes being the loss of innocence through the advent of war and the process of growing up. It did not quite work as a containing structure, but Hockney's designs lit up the whole of New York.

Within the year, the Met built on this spectacular success, with another triple bill devised by John Dexter, making Hockney famous as a stage designer throughout America. This was entirely devoted to works by Stravinsky: the early one-act opera, *Le Rossignol*, the ballet *Le Sacre du Printemps*, and the neo-classical oratorio *Oedipus Rex*. Hockney designed all three works but *Le Rossignol* was pre-eminent in its charm and spiky individuality. In 1983 London's Royal Opera House presented a double bill of *Le Rossignol* (in which Ashton's choreography for the balletic sections of the opera was memorably mimed and danced by Dowell and Makarova) and *L'Enfant*. Who can forget the theatrical magic of Hockney's special kind of chinoiserie in *Le Rossignol*, when a long shimmering silken scroll unfurled from the flies as the river, or the blue and white Ming of the Emperor's summerhouse and garden as it arrived on stage? In *L'Enfant* we could only marvel at Hockney's

inspired recreation of the world of childhood, both in the room with its timbered ceiling seen from a child's perspective, and in the enchanted garden at night – its frieze-like disposition of red trees influenced directly by the swirling linked figures in Matisse's *La Danse*.

In 1983 Ashton commissioned a backdrop from Hockney for *Varii Capricci*, his one-act ballet for Covent Garden to a short Walton score; the costumes were by William Chappell and the lighting by John B. Read. Characteristically, Hockney produced a swimming pool in a terraced Italianate garden loosely based on Walton's own garden and villa on Ischia; but the design seemed predictable and unremarkable. Hockney's most recent project was in 1987, designing – with great emotional panache in terms of colour and structure – Wagner's *Tristan und Isolde*, directed by Jonathan Miller, and conducted and performed by Zubin Mehta and the Los Angeles Music Center Opera.

During the past decade the Royal Ballet has commissioned more designs from painters than ever before, and here I must declare an interest, as I was appointed design consultant for opera and ballet in 1979. After Hockney's commission to design *Turandot* had been left unfulfilled in 1980, and hopes for Ashton commissioning Howard Hodgkin to design *Rhapsody* and Peter Blake to design a new production of *Nutcracker* had foundered, the policy of using painters as designers finally found its feet when Richard Alston was asked to choreograph a new work for the Royal Ballet. Alston selected the landscape painter John Hubbard to design a backdrop and simple costumes for his *Midsummer* ballet, set to the *Fantasia Concertante on a Theme of Corelli* by Michael

Tippett (lighting, John B. Read). Before working as a dancer and choreographer, Alston had studied art, and he has since sustained a close and unique contact with the visual arts. Hubbard produced a warm, semi-abstract evocation of southern landscape with stage and wings the colour of ripening wheat, perfectly reflecting the ripeness of Tippett's score.

Under Norman Morrice's guidance as artistic director, the Royal Ballet encouraged a younger generation of choreographers, and in 1984 new ballets were created by Michael Corder, David Bintley and Ashley Page. All were dancers – Page with the Royal Ballet, Corder and Bintley with the Sadler's Wells Royal Ballet – and eager to explore new ideas.

Corder chose music by Stravinsky, his short *Concerto in D*, and Patrick Caulfield as designer, instructing him to provide some kind of room for a party. The result was *Party Game* (lighting, John B. Read), a lively *divertissement* for a small group of dancers in elegant costumes against a brilliant backdrop which repeated the pink and red striped wall covering of the opera house auditorium, thus extending the pattern to the stage, where vast yellow painted lamps cast a painted circular yellow glow of light on the floor. The set is a great one, of historical importance.

247 **Party Game**, designed by PATRICK CAULFIELD (Royal Ballet, 1984)

Model photograph by Donald Southern

248 **Young Apollo**, designed by VICTOR PASMORE (Royal Ballet, 1984)

Production photograph by Group Three Photography Mark Silver (Apollo)

Bintley's ballet used Britten's short early work *Young Apollo*, with a specially commissioned score from Gordon Crosse, to extend and comment, in its own terms, on the Britten music. Bintley, attracted both by Pasmore's Apollonian abstract paintings and by the fact that he has lived and worked in the Mediterranean world for many years, commissioned from him backdrops and costumes. Undertaken in his eightieth year, this work was Pasmore's first for the stage. *Young Apollo* emerged as one of Bintley's brightest ballets. The Pasmore sets have purity and dignity: an expanse of white with a central circular blue pointilliste area with a linear drawn motif and a small orange disc to one side, the design looks timeless and has its own austere mystery. The simple white tunics and tights with black emblems for the dancers add to the mythical feeling as well as providing opportunities, on a white stage, for some of John B. Read's most subtle lighting.

Ashley Page created the third new ballet in 1984: *A Broken Set of Rules*, using a freshly commissioned score by Michael Nyman and backdrops and costumes by Deanna Petherbridge, with lighting by John B. Read. Page first explored music by Purcell before commissioning Nyman, who used some neo-

247

248

Purcellian themes in his ballet score which extend his music for the film *The Draughtsman's Contract*. Moreover, as Petherbridge's monumental drawings explore architectural fantasy themes, and as an amateur musician she also explores Baroque music, this collaboration was particularly well founded. Her luminous and spectacularly soaring architectural designs in black and white with austere grey costumes have great splendour. The ballet deserves revival.

Two new ballets followed in 1985: Jennifer Jackson's *Half the House*, backdrop by the abstract painter William Henderson, lighting by John B. Read and music by Bartók (the *Divertimento* for strings); and Michael Corder's *Number Three*, to Prokoviev's Third Piano Concerto, with sets and costumes by the American lyrical abstract painter Helen Frankenthaler, and lighting by Nick Chelton. For Jackson's ballet – with its warm, strongly rhythmical score partly derived from folk music – Henderson produced a powerful backdrop with semi-abstract intimations of a rural town with church steeple. For Corder's ballet, Frankenthaler created three abstract backdrops which caught and supported the contrasting moods of Prokoviev's sparkling score, but the design of the colour-stained costumes was not fully resolved.

249 **A Broken Set of Rules**, designed by DEANNA PETHERBRIDGE (Royal Ballet, 1984)

Production photograph by Group Three Photography

It should be said here that during 1985 the ballet press as a whole had found fault with the Royal Ballet's general standard of production and performance; this did not let up until Norman Morrice was replaced by Anthony Dowell in 1986. The policy of presenting new designs by painters was not helped by this negative situation. Although press reactions to the new designs were often enthusiastic, 1985 was a nadir for the Royal Ballet as a whole and the new designers suffered unduly. That time was equally inauspicious for a revival of Balanchine's *Ballet Imperial*, remembered as much for Eugène Berman's 1950 designs as for the choreography, and in 1985 given new designs by the distinguished painter, Christopher Lebrun. A romantic figurative artist, Lebrun produced an effulgently glowing set (lighting by John B. Read) – with banners draped over a classical square by a moonlit sea and sky – and equally sumptuous costumes. But the prevailing critical mood was not soothed by an unfamiliar spectacle when a familiarly sacred piece was expected. The production deserves revival in more supportive, less blinkered times.

By 1987 the Royal Ballet's new artistic direction was well rooted, so that Jack Smith's stunning backdrop and costumes for Ashley Page's *Pursuit*, to a score by Colin Matthews (*Suns Dance*) and lighting by John B. Read, received the acclaim that they deserved. Intensely musical in his grasp of abstract form, Smith designed sharply accented, vividly coloured shapes to drift or speed across the surface of a plain white ground, offset by equally brilliant costumes in striped or speckled patterns. The classical underpinning of the sharply plotted choreography is emphasized by flat disc-like tutus contrastingly coloured on both sides. The white wings and stage support the generally buoyant mood of the designs which also have historical importance.

In the preceding year Page had been invited to make his first ballet for what had in 1987 become, under Richard Alston's artistic direction, the Rambert Dance Company. He had chosen Jack Smith to design that ballet also, *Carmen Arcadiae*, to a Harrison Birtwistle score, with lighting by Peter Mumford. For this strong set, Smith designed a black

249

backdrop to contain bands of bright colour with the appearance of cut and collaged elements. Another ballet by Page for Rambert is *Soldat* – again with lighting by Peter Mumford – choreographed in 1988 to the Stravinsky suite devised from his longer *L'Histoire du Soldat* music; the sharply emblematic designs are by the performance artist and painter, Bruce McLean.

Opera's more conventional and practical needs, which usually preclude a more generalized or abstract approach, mean that opportunities for a painter to create designs for opera are more restricted than they are for ballet. However, Sidney Nolan did design *Samson et Dalila* by Saint-Saëns in a new production by Elijah Moshinsky in 1981 at the Royal Opera House, with many beautiful translucent scenes but with less convincing costumes. His 1987 collaboration with Timothy O'Brien on designs for Mozart's *Seraglio* opera seems impersonal, subdued beneath O'Brien's strongly structured concept.

From 1978 onwards Richard Alston re-established a tradition of using painters to design ballets from time to time at Ballet Rambert – initially as associate choreographer and then as artistic director. In 1981, as a foil for an unaccompanied solo dance for Michael Clark, *Soda Lake* – named after a mirage-inducing landmark in California's Mojave Desert – he used a striking sculpture by Nigel Hall, with suspended, apparently floating elements.

In the same year Alston asked Howard Hodgkin to design his first work for the stage: *Nightmusic*, to Mozart's *Notturni* for basset horns and voices, with lighting by Peter Mumford. Hodgkin's work as a painter has an intrinsic dependence on strong design and a compacted structure, and his first stage work, an abstract 'field' of colour patches, made a successful transition. But it was not until 1987 that Hodgkin was able to design a new production of *Pulcinella* to Stravinsky's great score, a commission intended for him back in 1981 but dropped, at my suggestion, because of existing plans to stage a different production by another company. For the 1987 *Pulcinella*, with new choreography by Alston, and Peter Mumford's lighting, Hodgkin's bold designs indicate not only the rough walls, houses and windows of the

Neapolitan setting, festively beflagged in the finale, but also a weirdly solid and passionate moon floating above the central, deep-blue nocturnal section. (The production was filmed by BBC TV in 1988.)

Robert North set high standards in design during his period as artistic director of Rambert, which preceded Alston's appointment. In 1981 he invited Bridget Riley to design his own *Colour Moves*, to a new score by Christopher Benstead, with lighting by John B. Read. Here North and Riley collaborated closely on a popular work which combined elements of choreography with Riley's astringently cheerful use of structured colour in the costumes and in five successive cloths.

In 1984 Richard Smith made striking designs for Alston's *Wildlife*, which used Nigel Osborne's music and lighting by Peter Mumford. Smith created a group of gently swirling and undulating kite-like shapes with coloured markings, set in spatial and polychromatic counterpoint to a wall-like backdrop, while Mumford's lighting achieved extraordinary feats of transformation. With the brilliantly syncopated and atmospheric music and Alston's fast-paced, delicate choreography, *Wildlife* must be seen as one of the best all-round collaborations of recent years. (This ballet was also filmed for BBC TV in 1988).

In 1986 John Hoyland was commissioned to provide a backdrop and simple costumes for Alston's *Zansa* (music by Nigel Osborne, lighting by Peter Mumford). Hoyland's own paintings are rich in colour with their own abstract 'situations'. For *Zansa* he managed to create a flowing design – with a strong red predominating – but which was cleverly structured to allow for spectacular lighting changes made through a spectrum of colour.

Alston also commissioned in 1989 Allen Jones to create set, curtain and costumes for his ballet *Cinéma*. This used the proto-minimalist score originally composed by Satie for Réné Clair's film *Entr'acte*, which was placed as an intermission between the two acts of the 1924 Dada ballet *Relâche*. Jones created simple, brightly coloured costumes and an austere black and white set with a lighting aperture as a trap for coloured light, and a keyboard to serve as a ramp for the dancers.

250

250 **Wildlife**, designed by RICHARD SMITH (Rambert Dance Company, 1984)

Production photograph by Catherine Ashmore Dancer, Lucy Burge

The sculptors Richard Deacon and Anish Kapoor, and the painters Stephen Buckley and John Murphy as well, all designed ballets for the Rambert's younger dancer–choreographers as an experimental venture during 1987–8.

The ENO in 1985 presented a new version of Offenbach's *Orpheus in the Underworld* with decor and costumes by the cartoonist Gerald Scarfe. Although the production was successful with the public, and everyone agreed that its visual impact was strong and inventive, for some it was too emphatically busy. In 1988 another cartoonist, Ralph Steadman, designed, with characteristic originality, *Dancing to Paint* at the Queen Elizabeth Hall, having four years before created a ferocious David Glass mime, *Crashed Car*, which toured widely. From earlier times, I must record here Osbert Lancaster's delightfully rural designs for Ashton's ballet *La Fille mal Gardée* in 1960, and buoyant port and shipboard designs for Cranko's *Pineapple Poll* in 1951.

This record of productions designed by painters may suggest that they have practically taken over the English stage. In fact they have designed only a comparatively small proportion of the total number since 1972, and have been restricted to ballet and, marginally, opera. Britain does have the most formidably gifted stage designers in the world, who can provide spectacle, technical innovation and particular refinements of design that are quite beyond a painter's grasp. Painters however, given the right teamwork, can and sometimes do provide an equally strong imaginative dimension on simple stage terms. In Britain, through the coincidence of Richard Alston's direction of Rambert and my own advisory role at Covent Garden, more celebrated painters have designed for the stage than in any other country in Europe, or in America.

The author is a critic, writer and broadcaster, and author of monographs on Jackson Pollock and Sidney Nolan. He was director of the Whitechapel Art Gallery from 1952 to 1968, and chairman of the Arts Council's exhibition committee from 1980 to 1984 when he presented the Dufy *exhibition at the Hayward Gallery.*

USING THE SPACE

Pamela Howard

Theatre can take place wherever there is a space for actors and an audience to meet: in church or on the street, in palaces or cafés, in attics or stadiums or exhibition halls, in hospitals and prisons, in a tent or the back room of a pub. The assumption, however – reinforced by the cultural habits of the past two hundred years – has been that theatrical performance properly belongs in a building specially constructed for that purpose.

In theory, such buildings extend the potential of theatre design, providing an ideal atmosphere of sound, light and space, sealed off from the distractions of the outside world. In practice, though, these buildings frequently confine theatre, wrapping it in an architectural cocoon, consciously or unconsciously designed to glorify established cultural and political attitudes. Too often, palaces of culture have proved cruelly expensive to operate, as well as artistically inflexible and unable to respond to changing needs and times.

Theatre people in recent years have sought out alternatives – less illusionistic, less conventional, often less costly environments in which to stage plays. In doing so, they have created not merely an alternative theatre, but also an alternative tradition of theatre design. Some of this work has happened in impromptu conditions or in temporary fringe venues; in other cases existing buildings with theatrical potential have been converted into theatres. The Riverside Studios, a converted recording studio in Hammersmith, and the Almeida, a converted chapel in Islington – both operating as arts centres – have unconventional performance spaces with strong architectural challenges. These have consistently inspired stimulating theatre design work. Similar

251 Ideas for suspension and flight were developed by the Station House Opera cast into **Drunken Madness – Invertebrate Living**, a piece presented in an old abattoir (London's Waterloo Studios, 1981). This was the start of a series of works created for specific sites. Here, the contrast between the chaotic surroundings of the building and the separate self-contained beauty of Station House Opera's construction is central to the performance. Designers: JULIAN MAYNARD SMITH and MIRANDA PAYNE. *Photograph by Rob White.* Seen are David Goulding, Klem Jarzabkowski, Julian Maynard Smith, Miranda Payne, Alison Urquhart.

252 Blood Group's production of **Dirt**, designed by KATE OWEN (ICA and other places, home and abroad, 1982) was Visual Theatre, a form using few words. The piece represented women and the sex industry, the bride and the whore. The central image was a large bed, a trampoline on wheels which tipped vertically for slide and film projections. The scenario was by Anna Furst who also directed, with lighting by Rick Fisher. *Photograph by Jill Posner.* From left: Anna Furse, Suzy Gilmour.

conversions include the Other Place in Stratford-upon-Avon and the Donmar Warehouse in Covent Garden.

Most interestingly, many of the major theatres built in the last twenty years have included, or expanded to include, small adaptable studio theatres. The Cottesloe at the National was designed expressly for that purpose, and the Pit at the Barbican (originally a rehearsal room) was altered to fill the same need. These studio theatres have produced some of the most ingenious and inventive design work of the past twenty years – no doubt because of the very limitations of their stages. In some cases the work presented in them has been so successful that it has altered the priorities of major companies. The excitement and immediacy of many RSC productions at the Other Place have also illuminated very clearly the difficulties of working in the company's main house, the Royal Shakespeare Theatre; and one positive result of these perceptions has been the creation of the Swan Theatre, a converted rehearsal hall now used to present the plays of Shakespeare and his contemporaries in an intimate auditorium.

The move from conventional theatres to alternative locations has challenged designers to confront, rethink, and act upon many of their profession's basic assumptions. Since the time of Gordon Craig and Adolphe Appia it has been axiomatic that 'by its nature, theatre is a spectacle to see and hear, and not a text to read'. In the context of alternative spaces, theatre design has been energized by the necessity both to assert the dynamics of the stage area, and to define the entire theatre space, its geometry and its relation to the spectators.

251

252

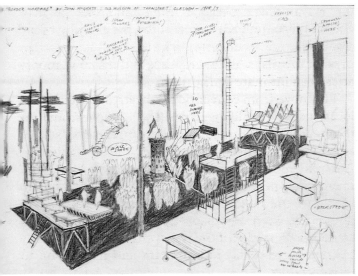

253

253 Pamela Howard's sketch for **Border Warfare** by John McGrath, telling the history of the England v. Scotland wars from 1200 to the present day. Designed specifically by PAMELA HOWARD for the Old Museum of Transport in Glasgow, 1988, the play – directed by John McGrath, lighting by Kris Misselbrook – starts in a primeval forest, later revealed as a football pitch. There were four mobile stages; audiences sometimes sat, sometimes promenaded; the entire building space was used; twelve actors and five musicians played six hundred parts.

In these circumstances, rigid hierarchical lines of demarcation between designer and director have had to give way to a collaborative common effort to invent spatially, and imagine three-dimensionally. The result, within alternative theatre, has been an enhanced creative role for the designer – in a very different sense from that usually associated with the mighty high-tech spectacles of 'designer's theatre'. It seems important not to neglect these less immediately visible, but perhaps much more revolutionary developments, when looking at the achievements of theatre design in the last decade.

How then do designers in the alternative tradition of 'poor theatre' approach the task of designing a theatre event? The process often starts with an assessment of the theatrical qualities of the given

254

space, or indeed a search for the kind of evocative building that could fit the event. In either case, the designer might first follow Craig's dictum to 'design with your feet as well as your eyes': by pacing the ground, feeling its size, its geometry. Work may then be done with a scale model, using scale figures to represent the actors. What the designer begins to discover is shared with the director, writer, actors, the composer and choreographer. The team becomes closely knit, working to exploit all the possibilities that are opened up to them, and that can infuse the text with fresh life and vision. The aim, as always, is to find the simplest way of telling a story, to help forward the actors' art, and to discover visual ways to touch the hearts and imagination of the spectators.

Productions conceived collectively and created for a specific space are, of course, deeply rooted there and not easily transferable. Any transfer or tour must be sensitively planned. Peter Brook's *Mahabharata*, which originated at his Bouffes du Nord in Paris, a gutted music hall, was recreated with enormous success in its nearest equivalent here, Glasgow's Old Museum of Transport. On the other hand, alternative productions are sometimes designed expressly to travel, and built to be adaptable to differing con-

254 The grand scale: Earls Court became a theatre holding 15,000 (June 1989) for a week of Bizet's **Carmen**, with a company of 500. In spectacular designs by STEFANOS LAZARIDIS, lighting by David Hersey, the audience sat in tiers round a sand-coloured bull-ring circled by a moving walkway of wood planks. Black-clad dancers were a kind of Greek chorus. Director Steven Pimlott. *Photograph by Clive Barda*

255 The final tableau of Framework's outdoor, dawn production of Aristophane's **The Birds** (Camden Lock, 1985), created by forty designers, painters, and performance artists with twelve actors. Rooftops were linked by a network of yellow ladders. Peter Avery directed, and adapted the text; lighting John Wyatt. *Photograph by Jean-Louis Gregoire.* Ona McCracken (Sovereignty), Marcel Steiner (Preisthataerus)

ditions. The Royal Shakespeare Company has from time to time given designers the freedom to design for a touring play a travelling set *and* auditorium complete, which can be put up within leisure centres or sports halls, thus enabling the productions to be seen in towns that do not have any theatre of their own. For the RSC tour of *The Taming of the Shrew* the director, Di Trevis, and I devised a production focusing on a small ensemble of actors, in which design and direction considerations were so deeply interfused that the play hardly appeared to be 'designed' at all in the usual sense. Yet in order to draw the audience into the play and make them feel its impact, much careful and detailed work had to be done to create the precise environment. The spectator who takes part in such a production should feel the text illuminated by the sheer physical presence and power of the actors, precisely because the physical qualities of the performers are a quintessential element in the design.

To the designer of alternative theatre the physical capabilities of the performers, how they use the architecture of the building to intensify a situation, and the significance of the props, are all crucial and interrelated elements. This emphasis on the power and expressiveness of the actor was well understood by Bertolt Brecht and his designer Caspar Neher, who together redefined the art of the theatrical performer as storyteller. Neher – a painter working in the theatre – knew precisely how to 'paint pictures with people', and create striking dramatic images on the stage by the most economical of means. To begin with, a good alternative theatre design might reasonably take the form of drawings or models showing different groupings of actors, these relating to one or more carefully chosen objects or stage emblems.

Above all, alternative theatre design offers an escape from the illusions and confinements of conventional theatre space. The outside terraces of the National Theatre were used to great effect in an early version of *The Passion*, the first stage in the evolution of Bill Bryden's *The Mysteries* cycle, with a text by Tony Harrison and designs by William Dudley. This production moved inside to the Cottesloe, and eventually on to a Rock venue, the dance floor of the old Lyceum Theatre, carrying its magic with it.

Shared Experience, the company formerly based in the studio of the Crucible Theatre in Sheffield, now work in an old laundry building in Soho. The tiny Traverse Theatre in Edinburgh, with a small, flexible stage, has challenged a succession of new artists and has produced clear, vivid, memorable designs. And, building on the success of Brook's *Mahabharata*, the Old Museum of Transport in Glasgow is to be converted for similar purposes on a permanent basis, giving Britain an alternative performance space of international stature, capable of accommodating major productions from abroad as well as initiating its own.

When members of an audience take part in a theatre event in a new and unconventional location there is a sense of excitement, an anticipation of a novel experience. They do not, as a rule, expect every detail of the story to be illustrated for them, nor for the stage to be filled with overwhelming evidence of a vast production budget: dazzling sets, magical props, sumptuous costumes. Paradoxically, the simplicity of many alternative stage pictures, following a different aesthetic, can produce a more powerful effect on an audience's sensibilities. Alternative theatre frequently reminds us that the play is indeed the thing. Once an audience's imagination is caught, it can with miraculous ease accept the truth of astonishingly unrealistic images. In *The Mysteries*, the Virgin Mary gathered an ordinary shawl carefully into a bundle and cradling just the rough material in her arms made the audience believe that it was the infant Christ, new born.

This oldest magic of theatre is finally its greatest strength. Freed from normal theatre conventions, exhilarated at seeing things played in unexpected spaces by performers with, often, transcendent skill, audiences are themselves transformed, capable of understanding more than they have heard, and of imagining more than they could possibly have seen.

As well as creating design for non-theatre spaces, the author designs plays for Britain's national theatres, and extensively throughout Europe and in the United States. She is also head of the theatre design department of London's Central School of Art and Design.

255

TIME FUTURE

Timothy O'Brien

Immersed in the present, familiar with the past, we aim our lights at the future, which reflects them like fog. Is something exciting hidden there for British theatre design? When the work of today is examined for clues to the future, an early conclusion is that very little is being done – as in all the arts – which was not present in some form early in the twentieth century. Technology has made execution easier and assisted a neo-Victorian populist fluency, but the interesting core of the art – its perceptions – evolves very slowly. The untidy reality of theatre design is that those who do it are skilled, and become more so as time goes by, but that their work has taken a long time to reflect developments in painting and sculpture; that they are to some extent insular and complacent, lacking a critical tradition which would help a truer valuation of their work; and that it would take something like a recovery of belief in life after death to make a difference that everyone would notice.

So what the future may hold is change in response to social rather than technical evolution, because theatre design is refreshingly unable to absorb a swamping amount of technology. Most high-tech productions attract attention as briefly as a firework display. That being said, improved light sources and computerized lighting control do add greatly to the language of design; and the adoption of unorthodox spaces for theatre creates more than a cosmetic shift in approach. Designers also have visual references at their disposal in unprecedented quantity; and the cinema has taught them that a story may be told through hints and startling juxtapositions.

In general, however, limited budgets and live audiences direct theatre designers towards theatrical reality, that is to say towards what can be done in the theatre and nowhere else. Theatrical reality is arbitrary and artificial. The powers of selective naturalism, abstraction or fantasy, are enormous. But the acquisition of these powers involves education. Until the mid-Fifties, many designers in our theatre emerged spontaneously, and began work without training or experience. Since then training courses have been fostered by inspired individuals like Margaret Harris of the famous design team, Motley, or by art schools. These have multiplied and produce about 130 graduates a year, so that by now hundreds of people have entered the professional pool, from which at any time maybe 250 are actively designing, up to 50 of them at a high level. The future is in the hands of a nearly-new profession. This breed is evolving a clearer sense of its identity, which leads to assertiveness. They possess the skill and daring to put on the stage what would have been dismissed as outrageous not long ago.

Oxford and Cambridge, just after the war, produced many of the people who have shaped today's theatre, and at that time they were intellectually nourished but visually starved; cut off from Europe and America, they profited from their own insular and literary tradition. Designers of that generation tended towards servitude, literacy, minimalism and were wary of foreign influences. They worked with directors, particularly directors of plays, who had an impulse towards small doses of design, fearing that more of it might not allow the performance to breathe or the words to speak; such directors could also be averse to visions which might limit their scope with actors in rehearsal.

But a new current in design has come in recent

years from opera, ballet and musicals, forms which are international, less dependent on the word, and reliant on vivid appearances for their fullest effect. Young opera directors and choreographers are becoming increasingly free and adventurous, willing to fly in the face of the expectations of the audience in an attempt to discover and highlight buried meanings. These newcomers have something to say, and develop a visual language to help them say it. This may involve neither the provision of predictable setting and clothes, offering a generally suitable atmosphere for the unfolding of the action, nor a capriciously chosen design style, which gives the appearance of adventure while sheltering a conventional production. Instead, content and meaning are underlined by a succession of telling images.

It seems paradoxical that the very conventions and stylized action of opera and ballet, governed by musical time and the preoccupying technical demands made on their performers, have enabled this thoughtful and adventurous design approach to prosper more than in the straight theatre. A reason for this paradox may be that actors in plays are freer and more eager to impose themselves on a production and, in this country, whilst paying tribute to the ideal of the acting ensemble, they acquiesce in the creation of stars. Our audiences love a sprinkling of stars; and stars are notoriously impatient of a theatre of ideas, in which design plays a strong part. But a large proportion of their public is now familiar with art in museums and galleries, which shows how communicative art and design can be without copying reality. We are beginning to catch up with the public abroad, for whom modern art is not a joke but a source of wonder. Modern art on stage, in the form of adventurous theatre design, is unsurprising, vivid and welcome.

Any future increase in the quality of theatre design in Britain will, when all is said and done, depend largely on the designer's relationship with his or her director, which is any designer's great concern. Designers and directors are necessary collaborators without being natural ones. Designers may ignore the directors' needs 'for the sake of appearances', and directors may imply that theoretical discussions are either a waste of time, bad form or – worse still – a trespass on their field. But the ideal for a director and a designer is to work together to engage the audience's individual imaginations, enabling performers to create from that audience one united response. Design is part of what makes people watching a performance understand and feel and so ask themselves questions and give themselves answers.

Despite this ideal, much of what will happen here will not be a triumph of the will – high-minded will at that – but a response to fashion. Look in the wake and designers may be seen bobbing about, flying the colours of past innovations: decorators to the high bourgeoisie; converts to Brecht, heavyweight realists who adapt his carts to greater axle weights but dump his ideological load; apostles of 'less is more'; adherents of a new romanticism; court painters to current society in the manner of Rauschenberg; those who see the benefit in an imitation of Joseph Beuys or a visit to the Tatlin Tower. The mix is rich. Recently a comfortable belief has grown up – deriving from prizes at international exhibitions and an insular view – that British theatre design leads the world.

But assessments of this kind are, to me, unsound and speculation on the point uninteresting. What is interesting is how far skill and perception and a sense of fashion can be combined in the design of productions that may tap everyone's treasury of feeling. We have our languages of speech, music and movement and of the eye; these, and our own memories, as we face the future, are all we have.

The author is a designer of plays and operas, principally for Britain's National Theatre, Royal Opera House and Royal Shakespeare Company. With Tazeena Firth he designed the musical Evita. *Abroad he has designed for the Comédie Française and the Vienna State Opera, among others. He won, jointly, the Gold Medal at Prague in 1975 for set design. Since 1984 he has been Chairman of the Society of British Theatre Designers.*

INDEX

Numbers in italics refer to illustration plate numbers

INDEX

INDEX